KRIEGIE

By
Robert L. Jackson

Printed by:
Johnson Graphics
P. O. Box 317
Decatur, MI   49045

FORWARD

We are brothers in the great fraternity that is infantry combat. We both earned the right to wear the most coveted award given by the United States Army. The blue bar with the silver wreath, the Combat Infantryman's Badge, was given to those who have heard guns fired in anger and responded accordingly in ground combat.

Robert Jackson, the author of this work, met the enemy in Belgium. My experience with an angry German Wehrmacht took place in Italy. The point is that I understand Bob's language and can walk in his combat boots as he weaves his story, retelling his experiences as a member of a rifle platoon.

Bob's description of the events leading up to the Battle of the Bulge in December 1944 is graphic. His continuing participation in that epic struggle is so crystal clear, the reader gets the feeling he is sharing the soldier's muddy foxhole.

The author's description of his killing, with a knife, one of Hitler's grey clad soldiers one night is written so well that the reader can feel the warm blood on his own hand. When reading about the gory deed, an indelible picture is etched on the mind. The description is so clear the reader, if called upon to do so, could repeat the act without difficulty.

Our soldier author takes us through each episode, step by step, slowly accelerating the excitement and our expectation until, like a roller-coaster, the apex of the story is reached and we are quickly dropped back to reality once again to wait until we start another exciting journey through the next true episode. This is story telling at its best and the stories Bob tells are fact, not fiction.

As my relationship with Robert Jackson unfolds, we plow more common ground together. We discover that both of us were in Camp Blanding, Florida during the spring of 1944. But our commonality extends to more than our shared experiences in the American Military. We were both raised in the northern part of the country. Bob hails from Michigan's Upper Peninsula town of Crystal Falls. I spent my formative years in Northern Wisconsin. Our outlooks and characters are strongly colored by this northern atmosphere. We both worked for the J.C. Penney Company. Bob's tenure was of long standing. I only waited on those who bought heavy woolen trousers and long underwear during the Christmas vacation from high school, but here again is a shared experience.

Based on my time on the line, Robert Jackson's descriptions of his adventures in combat are right on the money. His writing about his time as a prisoner of the Germans can be no less true.

Reading KRIEGIE takes me sharply back to the mud, gore and miserable times I experienced on the Italian front. I am, because his writing is so lucid, carried back and again feel the frigid blasts delivered by the weather gods, mixed with the bursting shells delivered by a much-hurt but largely undefeated Nazi Army. Because Bob's writing is as it is, the remembrance of the abject terror and fear comes back to me even though I sit warm and safe in my favorite chair, slowly turning the pages of a work that must be read if one cares to understand.

The author of this work deserves at least a Silver Star for what he accomplished in combat. I'm sure a decoration would have been his if his Captain, who initiates such things, had not suffered a mortal wound during the Battle of the Bulge. Recognition deferred, in this case, is recognition denied.

If there is any glory in war, let Robert Jackson have it now for giving us this splendid account of his experiences in battle and the suffering he, and others, endured in Germany as a prisoner of those who apparently had never heard of the rules of war as outlined in the Geneva Convention.

Ralph A. Casperson

Ralph A. Casperson
Captain Infantry Retired
Niles, Michigan
July 1995

KRIEGIE
(Kriegsgefangene)
Prisoner of War

The Germans called us "Kriegie;" we were prisoners of war. My chronicle begins in the Ardennes Forest and leads to our capture during the Battle of the Bulge. As the Third Reich violently lashes out in its final throes, forced labor camps impose starvation, humiliation and oppression on the P.O.W.'s. For 101 days I hold on to life when the reasons for doing so are not very clear and death beckons constantly.

Live with me in the foxholes. Experience the trauma of surrender. Endure the death marches. These frenzied months divulge the dilemma of the G I, the German citizenry and my brutal captors.

KRIEGIE tells little of the war's ostentation and pageantry. KRIEGIE's subject is, and must be, grim and terrible. Though prisoners of war are not criminals, often courage is our only fault and though our detention must not be considered as deserved punishment but as military necessity, nevertheless, all prisons and concentration camps are horrible.

The groans of men, one moment vigorous, the next shattered and broken by their guards, and the sight of strength visibly ebbing due to starvation and freezing temperatures are awful. It is the dark and cruel side of war that here must be told.

Therefore, I write a true story of a Kriegie so that generations will not forget that we live on the margins of an overly active and anxious world.

The Author

Chapter One

As I approach battle for the first time, an abrupt feeling of revulsion penetrates my thoughts. It pierces my understanding, making known to me that all of my basic training will soon be put to use. The shooting. The bombardments. The dirt. The killing. The survival.

With twenty other replacements, I am being sent to fill the empty slots in the squads of Hodges First Army, 28th Division, 109th Battalion. Many times these squads have been brought up to full strength, only shortly thereafter to be filled again--- and again. We are assigned to serve with veterans, in the battle of the Ardennes, who can show us the little tricks of self preservation they have learned since undergoing their first baptism of fire.

The ride in the personnel carrier to the jump off point is over deeply rutted roads. Our bodies are weary from the jolting and swaying of the conveyance, though we are gratified for the opportunity to ride rather than march. The carrier stops abruptly and we are commanded to keep silent and unload quickly. We jump off the back of the idling vehicle and then are summoned to form a semi-circle in front of the dim headlights.

I have been continually clicking the safety on my M-1 rifle with a nervous trigger finger. One of the veterans stares at me with a frank adversity as it annoys them when replacements are jittery.

We are each handed two extra bandoliers of clips and I find I do not know the correct way to place them across my shoulder so they will not interfere with the use of my rifle and gas mask. Glancing around I see that I'm not the only one who is having trouble with them. It is easy to pick out the replacements in the group. Even though it is a minor detail I wish my basic training had included this one small maneuver. It would have kept my morale from slipping.

Our dog tags have been taped together so they will

not jingle as we move and our gas masks are now taken away to be placed with the kitchen unit. The explanation? If we need them they will be brought to us! This doesn't seem logical but who are we to argue? Still, if the Germans use gas against us, a lot of American soldiers will lose their lives waiting for the kitchen unit to bring up our only protection.

In a matter of minutes we are formed into a single file and told to follow orders.

Our only order is, "Move out!"

Muscles tighten as we proceed with anxiety. Relaxation follows after half an hour passes.

Moving through the dense fir trees in the dark, occupies my mind as I listen to the swish of the branches as they tally each man in passing. A steep bank blocks our way and the forward progress of the squad is momentarily halted as each man struggles up the incline. As I stand and wait my turn, I realize how close we are to the front lines. Just ahead on the left sounds the rattle of a machine gun. It is soon answered by the cough of mortars, as shells explode and punctuate their reply. The machine gun, unnerved by the loud bursts, reprimands the mortars with a steady stream of fire, the staccato of its reply is final and the night retreats into its quiet.

At the top of the incline, a clearing spreads out before us and though we cannot see it, our leader informs us in whispered words that we are to hold on to the trenching tool of the man in front of us so we do not stray. The night is black without a star decorating its vastness. Each man breathes quietly, inhaling the cool air, pungent with the smell of pine.

Moving forward again as we play "follow the leader," it quickly becomes apparent that someone has lost contact with the man in front of him. We are wandering off to one side. The front man does not want to break the absolute silence we are commanded to observe and so we stumble around the uneven clearing like lost sheep. There is no panic and yet my heart is racing in unexpected anticipation.

The lead man trips a flare wire!

Suddenly an area as large as a football field is illuminated as the airborne flare bursts high above us, dripping its fire and smoke. It is as bright as midday in the clearing. I can see piles of rocks and tangled clumps of brush. Far to our right is the rest of the squad, hunched over, holding on to the man in front of them, still proceeding stealthily as though they are yet encased in the black of night. They quickly break rank and hit the ground while we still stare in shock and stand openly, inviting the light to show us the way.

A veteran swears softly and mutters, "Hit the dirt, you damn fools!" The commotion of getting into a prone position is enough to alert the enemy for five hundred yards around us. We are huddled up in a bunch where one well placed shell can wipe out the entire detail.

Again the voice rasps, "Spread out and keep down."

He starts moving along the ground by walking on his elbows, his rifle cradled in the crooks of his arms. He is heading for a pile of rocks and motions us to follow. Twelve men hit the dirt and race to keep up with him.

The flare burns out, blanketing us with a cover of eerie blackness. Now we cannot see the man in front of us and we are lost again. I wonder if we will ever get to the front lines, and if we do, will we be any kind of an asset to the Allied force? Men are whispering to each other, some trying to establish contact and others making sure they are not left alone in this dark clearing, one hundred yards behind the front fox-holes. The whispering is getting louder as the men try further contact.

A voice out in front of us commands, "Quiet!"

It is a clear voice and yet muffled. The whispering stops. Another command, "Listen men, the Germans will have that flare sighted in by now so we have to move fast. Get up and come directly to me."

The clatter of rifles against packs and ammunition is deafening in the wake of the muted voice. When he figures we are all around him, he again commands, "Grab contact and for Christ's sake hold on. Move fast and try not to make any unnecessary noises. We have to get to the command bunker before all hell breaks loose. Let's go."

No one breaks contact and as we tumble into the rear entrance of the command bunker, artillery shells are tearing the pile of rocks apart. This is our first performance on the battlefield. I'm sure our basic training officers would have blown their barracks bags if they could see their proteges profaning battle procedures.

The officer in charge of the bunker is raving madly, while we sit and listen to the front line language that is not unlike the words used in basic training. He is boiling! I cannot blame him. What a group to join his smoothly running company. He can see the days ahead as a nightmare that may give way to the whole German Army pouring through our ranks. He has nothing but a handful of veterans and the rest greenhorns to hold the area. After the tirade is over and he is out of words and voice, the group is separated into twos and sent to each bunker that dots the hillside. Lucky veterans that now hold possession of these holes in the ground we call home, now have the pleasure of seeing the men that have made such a dramatic entrance into this war.

After hearing grunts that take the place of a greeting, Roger and I settle in one corner and relieve our backs of the heavy packs. We have arrived! No one speaks and soon I am fast asleep, sitting on a muddy log in the corner. My call to guard duty, a few hours later, rudely enters me into the way of life on the front lines. For two hours I must stand outside the bunker, staring into the pitch black night, straining to hear sounds and searching for movements that never come.

The morning dawns while I am sleeping. One of my new bunker-hole partners shakes me to life and we start our daily routine of doing nothing while both our side and the enemy are content to hold the ground they now live in. We are far in front of our supply line and before any further progress can be made, the supply of food and ammunition has to be replenished.

I look over my new home and find it to be a hole in the ground eight feet wide and four feet from front to back. The depth varies as I step the length of the bunker. At one end, a hole drains the water accumulating from the dripping sides. Six poles are positioned on the floor to provide footing and to keep our feet dry. In the rear wall, two holes have been dug and the present occupants sleep there. Now the four of us will take turns. Straw sticks out of the openings and I wonder how they have procured it? The roof is about fifteen inches above ground level and consists of poles strung across a log framework that supports sod to give the appearance of natural ground from the air. The opening provides just enough room for a man to shoulder his rifle and fire from a standing position.

As I look out of the opening I can see what appears to be a network of twine strung on stakes in front of the bunker. It is about six inches off the ground and every fifteen feet an empty C ration can is suspended. There are rocks placed in a tight circle around the can. The network extends past the bunkers on each side for as far as I can see.

The purpose of this ingenious invention is for our protection during the night. If anyone tries to surprise us with a sneak attack, they will touch the twine and set the C ration cans jangling a tinny alarm. Not knowing where it is, they could hardly miss it if they are trying to move through it. If they walk, their foot will catch it and if they crawl, their helmet will come in contact with it. The slightest touch will set the can ringing. The veterans tell me the first night after installation, six cats were bagged. When the homemade alarm sounds, everyone starts spraying the area with lead, hoping to stop the intruder. It is a good example of what our officers mean about not straying beyond the bunker during the night. I make a mental note to listen to every word of caution that is passed down from the command bunker.

Breakfast is a cold meal of C rations, although we have our choice of K rations from the stock on the shelf that is the rear pole of the roof. "How long you guys been here?" I ask of the veterans.

"'bout a month, give or take a few days. Right, Pete?"

"Ya, 'bout that," Pete replies, shifting his weight from one foot to the other. "Riggins here joined me about then, I guess. There have been others in between."

The impression of his words tells me more than I desire to know. "Then Pete is the real veteran of this bunker," I think and store away the information.

"I'm Jackson. Bob Jackson, that is." Rising, I put out my right hand to Pete. He shakes it and acknowledges the introduction with a nod of his head. Then turning to Riggins, I shake his hand as he says, "Glad to meet 'cha."

5

Roger answers for me. "You mean you are glad to meet us after the commotion we caused last night? You must be awful lonely out here," he laughingly adds.

"Well, that was last night," Pete replies, "and today is today. That's how I look at it."

"Good. I'm Roger Korney and I'm sure Bob and I will do better from here on in." He shakes hands with Pete and Riggins and me. They are amiable fellows and the reception of the night before is understandable in light of the commotion we have caused. I know a man is never lightly treated if, by some careless action on his part, he draws fire to the others. There are no "dry runs" here. If you make a mistake you may never have a second chance to do better.

The morning passes without incident and I conceive a picture of war in my mind. If this is all there is to it, then I will pass with flying colors. Just before noon I am called to the command bunker.

As I enter the bunker, I observe seven men are present besides the officer in charge. He introduces himself to the new replacements as "Captain Ronnet," and then continues, "Men, we have some important work to do tonight. After last night's fiasco, I'm sure the Krauts will want to know what's happening over here. As you could tell by the incoming mail last night, they probably ALSO heard the noise you were making!"

He stands up from where he was sitting on the side of his bunk and walks to the center of the area. He sits on a box that serves as his desk. "They probably suspect either reserves or supplies are being brought up. If they knew the strength of this front line they would try a big push tomorrow. Tonight they will have a few patrols out trying to find any information that might help their cause. We have to stop those patrols before they get here. That is your job for tonight."

Pushing his helmet back on his head, he goes on, "I don't know where their patrols will originate or which direction they will start out to probe. All I know is that we have to stop them or at least give them the impression that we are knee deep in ammunition and men over here. I am issuing orders that the men in the fox-holes fire away at any sound heard in front of our lines. You men

6

will be out there so I must caution you to listen to every word I have to say."

All of us lean forward to listen to the strategy he has to offer. Sgt. Krigley is made leader of the detail and all orders will come from him tonight. We are to proceed to the edge of the woods and penetrate it to the depth we find best to set up our outpost. There we will form a firing line and wait for the patrols to come to us. We are to engage them with all the fire power we have and to turn them from their idea of scouting our rear positions.

A walkie-talkie will be in our possession but it will be used only in case of emergency. That is, if more than just a reconnaissance patrol is coming in the direction of our lines. It is very possible the Germans would take it upon themselves to send out a strong combat patrol to gain information. If this happens, we are to call for more men to join us and we are to spot for mortar fire.

I can see the men's faces. They are grimly set as they listen to the details of the plan. One false move by any of us out there could mean death to the others. The Captain explains this to the new men and tells us to watch the five veterans that will form the nucleus of the patrol. We should learn alot tonight if we prove capable of following orders and act like soldiers. We will leave the bunker with his words still ringing in our ears. This is to be the first test for the new replacements and it will also be a test for the veterans. It is up to them to show us the ropes, and if they fail it will be on their consciences for years to come. We are dismissed and leave the command post.

Returning to join Roger, Pete and Riggins, I sit in our bunker mulling over the details of the coming night's patrol. The others tell me I had better get some sleep if I am to be up all night. How can I sleep with all this on my mind? Yet, if I am to be wide awake and do my best tonight, I had better follow their good advice. I crawl into one of the holes in the wall of the bunker and as sleep is coming over me, I think of the dreaded detail of night patrol.

The command post just sent a message over the walkie-talkie to the bunkers. I am notified to report in fifteen minutes for patrol duty. I have been awakened from a restless sleep by being pulled bodily by the feet from my hole in the wall. A rude awakening, I think, as I sit on the pole floor trying to collect my senses.

The three men standing before me laugh at my sleepy face and Riggins jeers, "If Captain could see you now, he'd probably reject you for any patrol duty."

"I don't especially care if I go anyway. If you want to volunteer and take my place, I would just as soon go back to the sack," I yawn in reply.

Gathering my equipment and proceeding to the rear entrance of the command bunker, is interrupted by a series of more yawns. Five men are there ahead of me and I am told by the Captain to sit until the others join us. Sgt. Krigley is one of the two men we are waiting for. The Captain informs me, in almost fatherly tones, that Krigley is a good man and if I follow his instructions I will have nothing to worry about. I thank him and look over the other five men: three veterans and two replacements that look as green as I feel. The latter sit on the edge of a bunk, nervously fingering their wrist watches. Glancing up, they see me looking at them and a faint scared smile breaks the stiffness of their faces but it fades as quickly as it has appeared.

A commotion at the entrance draws our attention. Sgt. Krigley and another veteran enter. The briefing will start soon. I make up my mind to concentrate and absorb every word that is said.

Captain Ronnet places a map on the box in the center of the floor and lays a bandolier of clips across it to keep it from curling up. Placing his hands on his hips and spreading his feet, he starts, "You men remember what was said this afternoon about the purpose of this patrol?" Looking around to make sure we all nod our heads, he goes on. "Listen carefully now so I don't have to repeat. Sgt. Krigley will be in charge and all orders will come from him. He will handle the radio and use it only at his discretion. Cpl. Watts is second in command and in case of emergency he will take over. Is that clear?"

Again our heads bob in approval. As he fingers the curled corner of the map, we edge closer to get a better view. "The top of this hill we are on, is level, extending three hundred yards to the left and approximately one hundred yards to the right. The company flanking us on the left, meets ours at the crest of the slope three hundred yards from here. We are not exposed on that side, however, we are exposed on the right. Our company area ends at the crest of this hill on our right, approximately one hundred yards from here." Throughout all of these explanations, he is pointing to the positions on the map.

"The next company is down in the valley and a gap of a couple hundred yards separate us. The Krauts don't know this or they would be probing that area constantly. They haven't done this as yet according to our reconnaissance. We have to assume they will investigate this area considerably tonight after the commotion in the center of our company last night."

I feel the back of my neck turning red and I hope we will not hear any more about last night. This really puts us three replacements in a hot spot with the five veterans. If it wasn't for our bungling last night, this patrol might not be needed tonight. What a pleasant thought! Three green men that know nothing of combat, going out on combat patrol with a bunch of veterans who hold our very existence against us.

The Captain continues, "You men must locate their patrols tonight and give them hell with everything you've got. It will confuse them and change their plans as to coming any closer to our front lines. They may think you ARE our front lines and figure they miscalculated their forward movement. I don't care what you do, as long as they are exposed and given a healthy welcome. They must report to their superiors all kinds of different information. You have to plan to be on the move all night. If you stop one patrol and turn it back, get out of there quick because they will zero in their mortars on you when they get back to their lines. You men will stay out there all night until there is no more chance of them sending out patrols because daylight would show their movement. That's an order!"

The veterans shuffle their feet and sit back on the boxes. As the Captain points to a spot on the map, they lean forward again. His finger touches the map where two lines have been drawn in heavy black pencil. "This is

9

a small gully that could afford protection for you if you get in a tight spot. The Germans know about it too and so be careful if you use it. You men that were here a week ago remember when we cornered that Kraut patrol there. If they had stayed there only five minutes and regrouped and got out of there, they would have been safe. They chose to stay and fight it out and our artillery knocked them out with three shells. Remember this if you have to use it for an emergency. Actually, it would be better if you give it a wide berth."

As he takes the bandolier off of the map, it curls up into a tight roll. Then he snaps an elastic band around it and asks, "Any questions?"

Sgt. Krigley speaks up. "Can we call for reserves if we need them, Sir?"

The elastic band snaps again on the parchment paper. He turns to put it on the shelf above his sleeping bag. No answer. He turns slowly, fingering his chin. The deafening pause in his speech paralyzes us. He answers, "No."

His words break into my thoughts, "If you can't rout any patrol out there, then start moving around, lose contact with them and attack again from another position, stick together and throw alot of lead around. They will soon become discouraged. Your fire power should be as great if not greater, than theirs. Hakket will have his BAR and that should keep then on the run. "He strides over to the other side of the bunker, trying to form words that will be of use to us in case we really get into a tight spot. "I'm ordering you to stay out there all night with no reinforcements for this reason: if I call any more men from our line, it will weaken us too much. You have heard that men are expendable? Well, in this case, I'm relying on Krigley's leadership and all of you working together to pull through this. Your actions tonight may be responsible for saving thousands of lives. If the Germans know how thin our lines are here, they might start a big push. Yet, if I take any more men out to help you, we would not be strong enough to stop any kind of an attack, let alone a big one. In other words, you men have an important job to do tonight and you must do it alone. I can't give you any more help so use your heads and give them hell." He picks up his helmet and places it on his head. The pistol belt is clamped around his waist and he leaves the bunker. The briefing is over as far as he is concerned!

When he is gone, I turn to Sgt. Krigley and ask, "What in the hell did he give us a radio for if we can't call for help?"

The Sergeant grins, a warming smile coming over his grizzled face, "We're to use it to report information to him as to our contacts and position. We will use it alot tonight if things get tough. We can call for mortars to blast an area in front of us if we need it. Also, if we can give them the approximate number of men in the enemy patrol, they will know how to handle them if they get around us."

"Or through us," I mutter.

"They won't get through us!" he snaps angrily. "Listen you guys, we are going to make out alright tonight. We won't give up no matter what happens. Get it?" His piercing eyes survey the group. "Keep firing until your rifle barrel is red hot! Don't stop! And when it's so hot it won't fire, then throw grenades while you wait for it to cool. Don't lose contact with the group whatever you do. Like the Captain said, 'Use your heads and follow orders.'" His sincerity in believing his own words bolster us and I know the patrol as a whole will make out alright. Whether all of us will make it back alive is another question.

"O.K. - let's prepare to move out. You new men come over here and I'll show you a few tricks that may help you tonight." We cross over to him as he stands up. Without a word he stoops over and reties his shoes. Small bow with the loops and ends tucked in so they won't catch on anything. I notice the other veterans are doing the same.

Next comes the leggings. We take our leggings off and pull our pants tight at the ankles. We tie these tightly in place with the supply of shoe laces on the floor, winding the lace around our leg half way up to the knee and knotting it there. The heavy canvas legging would make alot of noise as we walk through the brush.

Everything from our pockets is emptied in neat piles on the floor. Sgt. Krigley picks out the things for me to put back: my pocket knife and an OD handkerchief. That

11

is all! My wallet, comb, cigarette lighter and other things are not to be taken. "Too much noise and bulkiness," he says.

Cartridge belts are loosened and checked to see if they are full, then wrapped around our waist after we have tucked in our shirts tightly under our belt. He grabs my cartridge belt, shakes it, and me with it. A faint "clink" emits from the movement. He shakes me again. "Clink, clink."

"Let's see your pocket knife," he orders.

I produce it and wonder what he is going to do. Opening it, he cuts the metal end off of my belt and hands back the knife. The end of the belt might unravel but at least the noise is gone.

Next comes the OD shirt sleeves. There are two buttons on the cuffs. We button them to the tightest fit so the sleeves will stay down and not expose our white arms; it keeps the sleeves tight and will not be as likely to catch on branches. Cigarettes come out of the shirt pockets and join the neat piles on the floor. There will be no smoking out there tonight.

We unbutton our shirts to check the tape holding our dog tags together. They make alot of noise if left loose. Our helmet straps are brought up and over the front of the brim and snugly fastened. Back packs are not needed, only the first aid kit on our cartridge belts.

We jump up and down individually to see if any noises are made. I can't see how we could miss anything but it is possible. When Cpl. Watt's turn comes, he jumps up twice and his cartridge belt clatters to the floor. He looks in surprise as he bends to retrieve it. Buckling it on, he jumps again. The belt falls once again. Evidently the catches are worn. Sgt. Krigley gets another one for him from the pile of new ones in the corner. After a few minutes of adjusting, Cpl. Watts is again up with the rest of us.

Our rifles are next on the agenda. Slings are pulled as tightly as possible so they won't jingle against the barrel. Sgt. Krigley holds his in front of him and shakes it fiercely. No noise. My turn next. At the first shake, a noise like a bell comes out of the stock. My jaw drops at the unexpected sound. It is the repair kit that is nestled in the stock behind the butt plate. I reach in my pocket to get a penny to loosen the screws. Finding none, I remember they are in the pile on the floor. I pick one up and take off the butt plate. The tool falls out in my hand and I wrap it in a piece of cloth that one of the men hands me. With the tool packed in the stock again, I replace the butt plate and put the penny in my pocket.

Sgt. Krigley's voice flatly states, "Put it on the floor. There aren't any PX's out there."

I know my face turns red as the others laugh. He slaps me on the back, "Don't worry, soldier, you'll make it. That's just an example of forgetfulness that could do the whole bunch of us alot of harm tonight. Keep on your toes and think before you act." Crossing the room, he says, "Let's get our make-up on, soldiers."

The top of the small heater provides us with the black soot to cover our hands, faces and necks. When we finish, he gives each of us a GI compass, complete with case to attach to our cartridge belt. Next comes our supply of ammunition, no specified amount, just what we can carry. I take three bandoliers loaded with clips and also three hand grenades. I am a walking army. Our bayonets and scabbards have been taken off earlier and a trench knife is substituted for it. We are ready.

Before leaving the comparatively safe positions of our front lines for the wooded area ahead of us, we check our compasses. After orienting our positions in our minds, we fall in behind Sgt. Krigley as he moves out into the darkness. Cpl. Watts brings up the rear and we three greenhorns are safely placed in the middle where the veterans can keep tabs on us. Second in line is Hakket with his BAR, ready to direct his fire power under Krigley's orders.

It seems different tonight, moving through the darkness into an area I don't know. There is no need to hang on to each other to keep together as we did last night. It is pitch black out yet I seem to have gained a sixth sense. Somehow I can feel the other men's presence and I wonder if in the past few minutes I have become a veteran, a man who has finally gained self confidence in himself and can be depended upon to serve as a member of a team. No individualism is wanted here; everyone must work together.

13

We move silently out of the grassy clearing and into the woods, rifles at port arms are ready for any action that might confront us. The direction we take is straight ahead of our front lines. Threading our way between the trees and bushes, we move slowly and noiselessly forward, pausing every few minutes to listen for sounds that will warn us of an approaching enemy patrol. If they are moving as quietly as we are, they might be on the other side of the huge tree I am passing and neither of us will be aware of it.

Each step is a separate event as we place our foot on a branch and quietly remove it until a soft footing is found. Then, as the body moves up a step, branches and brush are quietly held aside and let back to their normal position so as not to create a swishing noise. This tedious job is slow but very important to the success of the patrol. We have to get far enough out in front of our lines to intercept the enemy before he gets too close. We have to detect him first, otherwise he may go around us and set up an ambush instead of us giving him the surprise. They wouldn't expect to make contact with us so far ahead of where they think our positions should be and the element of surprise could balance the coming battle if they outnumber us. We have moved forward approximately four hundred yards when Sgt. Krigley gathers us into a huddle. He whispers so low we can hardly hear him.

"Form a skirmish line to the left and right. Four men on each side, twenty-five yards apart. When you reach your spot, find cover, lay perfectly still and listen for them to come. They won't be too cautious this far in front of our lines. If you hear them, signal the men on either side of you by lightly patting your rifle stock two times. Pass the signal on and start moving toward the man who signaled. When you are close to him, find cover and wait for Hakket to open up with the BAR. Then give them everything you've got, even if you can't see them. Fire away until I pass the word along to stop. Then move back and to the right about fifty yards. We will regroup there and make our next move."

"If they start running, follow them up for awhile, don't go too far, come back here and join the others.

14

Any signal for movement, other than my commands, will be two pats on the rifle stock. Be perfectly quiet when you're not moving and listen not only for them but also for the signal to regroup. No hand grenades until they are really needed. Save them for an emergency unless you can plainly see the Germans against the sky. Get it! While you're moving out I'll report to the Captain on the walkie-talkie. Good luck and remember, keep your wits about you. We can't call for help and yet the patrol must accomplish this mission. O.K., move out."

Another replacement and I move to the right with Hakket and Watts. First Hakket positions the other replacement, then stops off after the next twenty-five yards. I continue on to my cover while Watts moves to the flank. I find a small gully almost like a slit trench that is just deep enough to provide cover and yet give me a view of the area. It sees perfect and I slide into position, propping my rifle in front of me. Watts has just left me and I know he is moving but I cannot hear a sound. I loosen my helmet to give my ears a better chance to hear. All is quiet.

I strain my ears to hear noises and after ten minutes I decide to relax and conserve my strength. Who knows, I may be in this position all night. Maybe they won't send any patrols out! The thought brings a smile to my face. It vanishes when I think that I will probably be sent out here again tomorrow night. No, if they are going to come, let them come now.

I banish all thoughts from my mind as I concentrate on listening for telltale brush cracking or the signal from our patrol. The clouds above seem to part more frequently now and the moon gives an eerie glow to the woods. I can faintly see the outline of trees and bushes before me. Forty-five minutes pass and as I continue to listen and look I find I can see better as the moon rises higher in the sky. I slide a bandolier off of my shoulder and place it alongside my rifle with the clips in readiness for quick action.

Suddenly as I look into the grey scene ahead of me, I think I can see a shadow moving. I raise my hand to tap my rifle stock for the signal. I stop it in mid-air! "Have I been seeing things? Is it just a figment of my

15

imagination after staring so hard?" I find myself tense
and my eyes are in a squinting strain. Trying to relax
is difficult and yet if I am to see clearly, I have to
compose myself. Again the shadow moves, followed by
another. They are about sixty yards in front of me and
coming in at an angle. If they proceed as they are, they
will come right between Hakket's and my position.

"Good deal," I reflect, "we have them figured right.
That is Sgt. Krigley has." Raising my hand, I softly yet
solidly tap the rifle stock twice. Then listening to see
if it has been loud enough, I faintly hear Hakket passing
the signal on. Turning my attention back to the ghostly
looking shadows threading their way through the trees,
I try to count them. Picking a clear spot between two
bushes, I count six men. "That's not bad," I ponder, "we
surely can handle them." They pause and I count three more
moving forward to catch up with them. Nine against eight
so far. The element of surprise will even that up in a
hurry. "Let them come."

I hear a twig break and I have to smile. They aren't
expecting any welcoming committee if they are traveling
that noisily. Now I can hear their footsteps plainly as
they cross a rock strewn area. Knowing the enemy is
approaching and being prepared for them, calms me. The
sensation I feel is not hatred. It is the awareness of
the hunt and I find it sharpens my senses, the same as
waiting on a deer post as a big buck approaches.

Then a noise at my side brings the sweat out on my
forehead and makes my heart pound hard. I turn to see Sgt.
Krigley a few yards away. He crawls alongside of me and
with his mouth to my ear, whispers, "Where are they and
how many?"

I exchange head positions with him and answer, "Right
there," as he sights along my outstretched arm. "Nine of
them are all I can count."

"Good work," he says. "I can see them as plain as
day now. They can't see us on the ground so don't worry.
Wait for Hakket to open up. I'll be with him. Where is
Watts?"

"I don't know. He should be here by now. You came
twice his distance."

"He'll be here any minute now," he assures me. He

looks over to the right side in front of us. "When he comes, tell him to take a position behind that windfall over there. He can give us flanking fire and still not be too far out in front."

Looking back at the enemy patrol, we notice they are almost in the same spot as before. They start moving again and after about fifteen yards they stop. Krigley studies their movements and shakes his head. "Poor buggers, they sure are going to get a surprise."

He moves out toward Hakket as quietly as he has come. I know we are in good hands just by watching him slither along the ground making good progress and not making a sound. He has to get back and move Hakket closer to me and also place the other men. I look to the right, trying to locate Watts. He is nowhere in sight.

It seems like an eternity waiting for the Germans to come into our ambush. When they are only twenty yards in front of us, Hakket lets them have it. The rest of us fire almost simultaneously and the salvo cuts down the first four men. The other five drop to the ground and start firing in our general direction. They have been taken completely unaware and we continue pouring lead into the area where they "hit the dirt."

Sgt. Krigley hollers out, "Fire away and move forward, get them on the run."

I empty my clip and it pops out as the rifle ejects it. Quickly I draw one from the bandolier and ram it into the waiting chamber. Hakket is pouring a continuous stream of fire at them and they have little chance to return the fire as they huddle undercover. I can hear Watts firing from his first position, twenty-five yards to my right. A grenade explodes and we know that he has tied into another group and is holding them off by himself.

Krigley shouts, "Hakket, you and the end man go up and help Watts, we can take care of these men. Hurry up now and give them hell until we get there."

Hakket joins me and we move in a crouch toward the right. Watts is firing as fast as the Garand will allow him, stopping only for fresh clips. As long as the firing continues we know he is alive and holding his own. It will take the German patrol only a few minutes to figure out there is only one man in front of them. If we can

17

only get to him in time we can change all that, especially when Hakket opens up with the BAR. Hakket leads the way and we circle in back of Watts' position, approaching the skirmish that is one-sided. Evidently the Krauts have sent out two patrols to come through at the same time. One hit our patrol in the center while the other has just come within Watt's range. Watts engages them rather than letting them get by us. He has guts. Imagine taking on a whole patrol by himself! He hasn't a chance unless he can move around and confuse them. But he cannot move. He has to protect the flank of the patrol.

Now we are to the right of Watts. Just as we take our positions, Watts sees us and shouts, "Give 'em hell, men. Here they come!"

The Krauts have figured out that Watts is alone and they are going to rush him. There are six of them and they jump up at a command from their leader. They sound like a bunch of wild Indians coming through the trees. As they run forward they fire without aiming, hoping to keep Watts pinned down until they are on top of him. I see Watts rolling over on his side and his arm flings a grenade directly in their path. Hakket and I raise up and pour a withering cross fire into their ranks. Their shouting stops. Completely demoralized, they turn and run for cover. Two of them make it and disappear into the eerie grey blend of trees.

Watts jumps up from his position and runs toward the supposedly dead enemy, rifle ready for any tricks they might try. We join him after viewing the scene with no feeling of moral fright from killing these men. We look at Watts' smiling face as he says, "Thanks boys, I didn't think I had a chance until you joined me." Shouldering his rifle, he turns from the grim scene and says, "Let's report to Krigley, I don't hear anymore shooting going on over there."

We follow through the grey light, winding our way back to the meeting place behind our original positions. The rest of the men are there waiting for us. Sgt. Krigley steps forward to greet us and in a muffled voice asks, "Anyone get hit?"

"Yeah," Watts says, "Four Krauts. Two more got away."

The Sergeant's look of anxiety vanishes as he finds

us without a scratch. The others have made it without casualties also. The first German patrol was completely wiped out.

Joining the ring of men around Krigley for further orders, we feel strong again in the presence of a full strength patrol. The Sergeant advises us. "Don't get cocky over our first victory tonight. You might get careless. Remember that one patrol almost got past us and we had the element of surprise on our side. From here on, it promises to be a rough night."

We follow Krigley as he leads us to the right and out of the area. He expects the German artillery to start blasting this area in a few minutes because the two Krauts that have made it to safety, will report to their headquarters. We move to the area where there is a gap between our company's end position and the flanking company down in the valley. This is dangerous territory, as movement so close to our lines, is liable to draw fire from our own men. Using his compass to guide us, Krigley is as stealthy as the movement of an animal whose very life depends on not being heard or seen.

Slowly and quietly we match his stealth and gain the crest of the hill and regroup. It has taken an hour to move these few hundred yards and now it is almost 2 A.M. The moon still gives us enough light to distinguish trees and stumps from moving men. It is perfect for patrol work and the Germans will take advantage of it. Last night had been as dark as could be and these clearer nights are few and far between.

The last half hour of stillness has been punctuated by loud blasts of German artillery, probing the area we have just vacated. There is not as much artillery as we have expected but then it only takes one shot if it is a direct hit. It reminds us of our hazardous job as we lean forward to hear our new orders.

Sgt. Krigley declares, "If the Germans send out a patrol on this side tonight, they will follow the ridge. We're going to fan out at a thirty degree angle with the ridge in view of every man. Two men will be posted on the edge overlooking the slope. They are the point of the trap and must hold their position at all costs, while also watching down the slope which will be the only choice of retreat to the enemy if we get him on the run. The signals are to be the same as before: two taps on the rifle stock means to tighten the trap around the Germans. No one will fire until Hakket opens up with his BAR and grenades will be used only in case of emergency."

We settle down in our positions to wait. The air is cold and damp. As it penetrates our bodies in the prone position, muscles become cramped and minds become dulled. An hour passes, two hours; it is now four o'clock and the moonlight is dull from the early morning mist that fills the air. Visibility is cut considerably and spirits are down as we wait impatiently for the enemy to show himself.

Listening carefully, we can hear one of our men moving his legs to get the circulation started. A few more minutes pass and suddenly the clatter of a rifle against a steel helmet jolts us from our drowsy watch. One of the men at the point has fallen asleep and his head has moved sideways as he relaxed. His helmet fell off and clanged against the steel barrel. Its sound rings through the night and anyone within a half mile could hear it. Two taps on a rifle stock sounds from the Sergeant's position as he signals a regrouping. We struggle to our feet with aching muscles and half closed eyes and move toward him.

Rifle fire breaks out in front of us!

Hitting the dirt and rolling over to gain new positions, our rifles return the fire and bring us out of our stupor. It is agonizing to realize that a German patrol has been proceeding along the ridge under the cover of the mist, and because of the known fate of their former patrols tonight, has proceeded exceedingly cautious to avoid the same fate. In a few minutes they would have walked right into our trap but were notified instead by our carelessness. Evidently the Germans have sent out a stronger patrol and they are loaded to fight. Burp guns and machine pistols riddle the trees and brush in front of us. It is easy to deduce that we are outnumbered in both manpower and fire power.

Since it is the purpose of our patrol to give a show of strength we settle down in our cover and give forth with a continuous firing rate. The burp guns and other automatic weapons the Krauts have, are not very accurate and since the Germans are known for their comparatively poor shooting, we have only to keep down and return the fire as they cannot tell if we are firing heavy or not. We bide our time and fire at the blinding flashes coming from their guns. As I load another clip into my rifle, I attempt an approximate count of their men. As near as I can conclude from their firing positions, there are about twelve to sixteen men, almost twice the size of our patrol.

Since I am second from the end again with Watts on the extreme end, I can get a full picture of the scene. We have the best position with the woods behind us. The Germans have their backs to the ridge and their only way out is down the other side. If they stand we will see them silhouetted against the sky and we have a partial cross fire on them now.

Sgt. Krigley calls to me from behind my position. Letting me know who he is before trying to gain the perimeter of my position, probably saves his life. I am not going to take any chances on the Krauts encircling me. He crawls up to me and whispers in my ear, "Follow me. I'm going to pick up Watts and tighten the noose around them. Our only chance is to press them and make them take off down the slope. The two men on the other end have orders to hold their positions at all cost and if we anchor down this side and the men in the middle move in, I think we can make then run." He lifts his head up then adds, "Keep your trench knife in your hand as we move forward. They may have a few reserves in back of them along the side where we are going. The man next to you is already pulling over and forward to cover this area. Let's go."

He makes it sound so simple and yet I know I am in the thick of the worst battle I can imagine. I would just as soon dig a hole in the ground and wait for the skirmish to end but not wanting to be left alone in this spot, I turn and crawl after him. With bandoliers of ammunition clutching at every rock and root on the ground, my rifle cradled in my elbows and my trench knife in my hand, I follow Sgt. Krigley as he slithers ahead of me. He is a master at the art and I, a scared beginner.

As we near Watts' position, Krigley signals him before approaching his side. After a few whispered orders, Watts motions me to fall in behind the Sergeant. He will bring up the rear. I ask myself, "Why have I, a novice, been

21

in the same spot two times tonight? I have to go on extra duty while the men who know how to handle this much better than I are left behind to cover our movement!" It seems all wrong to me and the only comfort I gain is from the fact that I am with two good men. "Small comfort," I think. "One mistake on my part and I will snafu the whole strategy."

We move in a small semi-circle and through the mist of dawn's light, I can see the crest of the hill which is to be our objective. Ten more minutes, I figure, and this tortuous crawling will be over. Sgt. Krigley halts and his hand motions for us to stop and lay still. "What is happening now to interrupt our plans?" At least it gives me a chance to rest. He motions again, this time to his ears as he points ahead.

Lifting my steel helmet away from my ears, I can hear the muffled whispering of a foreign language. There are Germans right in front of us, just a few feet away, having an argument! They are almost twenty yards from the German firing line and their presence here irks me. I wonder, "Will we have to crawl around them? Does this mean the Krauts have reinforcements all the way back to here? That adds up to at least twenty-five men! If so, why aren't they committed or are they supposed to circle around behind our patrol and cut off our escape?"

I know Sgt. Krigley will have the answer. He moves back on his elbows and toes until he is alongside of me. Watts moves up to joins us. Krigley ponders for a moment and cupping his mouth to our close heads, whispers, "I figure because they want information instead of a fight, these two in front of us are the rear guard of the patrol. That's why they are this far behind their other men. From what I can understand of their arguing, one wants to leave now with the information and the other wants to stick it out for awhile and see how their patrol makes out. I would like to let them go and report that we have this area protected but they are in our way now. We will have to get rid of them quietly. We don't want our movements revealed to the rest until we are in our positions and ready for them." Looking at me he says, "You had any training in knife fighting, soldier?"

I gulp then shake my head sideways.

"You will have to learn in a hurry then because you and Watts will have to get them while I go to the ridge. Don't fire your rifles. If they fire at you, I have to be up on the ridge to stop their men from stampeding out of the trap they will know is being set for them."

He looks ahead then turns to us, "Give me a couple minutes to get started and then close in. In the meantime, Watts will give you a few basic rules. Follow them. You won't get a chance to try again. Good luck." He crawls to the left and in a few seconds disappears into the scenery without a sound.

Watts is shaking his head and whispers in my ear, "I can't teach you anything in a minute!" I can see sweat coming out on his forehead as he speaks. Holding his trench knife out in front of him with the blade pointing up, he whispers, "Hold it this way, not with the blade down. It's easier to defend yourself with it this way and an upward stroke works better than a downward one. When we go for them, try to get behind your man and with your left hand reach around and grab his mouth or throat. Your right hand should put the trench knife below his ribs. Keep the blade flat and keep punching until you know your job is done. Get it?"

I nod but really didn't "get it."

"My rifle! What should I do with it?" Before I can ask, Watts says, "We'll take our rifles with us and leave them only at the last second. If they are still talking when we get close to them, we will have a better chance. Naturally they will be facing each other, so you will take the one whose back is to us. I'll get the other. They don't know we are around so the odds are in our favor. I'll go first; you keep tight on my heels and don't make a sound."

"How can he be so callous as to think I won't make a sound?" My head is shaking inside my helmet, my heart is pounding against my ribs and I know the Germans will hear me. When he moves forward, my elbows and legs refuse to answer my call for motion. Only with superhuman effort am I able to get them working. They are like lead weights holding me back.

We gain the fringe of bushes and can clearly hear the Germans whispering. So far, so good! If they had

23

heard us they would be quiet now and watching for the source of the noise. The firing of the two patrols locked in combat only a few yards away seems unimportant to me. They are shooting at shadows and stumps that look like men and here we are not six feet away from two Germans who are to be our victims. They are squatting down with their heads together, gesticulating with their hands, rifles laid at their sides as they argue. Watts looks at me and quietly lets his rifle slip from the cradle of his elbows to the ground. I do the same and take a firm grip on the trench knife handle as we rise to our feet. The thin tangle of bushes that separates us from them is about three feet high and gives us no trouble as wejump forward to silence their arguing voices.

I can see Watts flying past my shoulder to land on top of his man as I grab and thrust. There are no feelings of regret or remorse as I concentrate on what I am doing. Strength seems to surge into my arms and legs as I throw the German to the ground - a lifeless form. Blinding lights seems to be flashing in my head and I sway as the stillness of inaction sweeps over me. I regain my thoughts when I see Watts pick up a pad of paper on the ground and motion for me to follow him.

We pick up our rifles and rejoin Sgt. Krigley. My head is swimming in unreal thoughts as I realize what has just happened. I lay beside two whispering men as each reports on their actions of the past few minutes. The time has come to close the trap and force the enemy patrol out of their positions and down the slope.

It is beginning to get a little lighter now and we can see their shadowy forms as they raise to fire their automatic guns. Crawling close to tighten the circle before firing, we notice their firing has slowed down and it is probably from having their ranks thinned by our men's more accurate fire. We can see each one of them raise up and fire a burst of lead without aiming. Their bullets are at least four feet off of the ground by the time they reach our men's position.

Meanwhile, their automatic weapons are being answered by sharp reports as our Garands spout 30 cal. bullets close to the ground around them. I admire the Sergeant for having guts enough to take the initiative and not admit defeat.

As I look over at him, I can see a slight smile on his face as he realizes the plan he has so quickly formulated is working to the best of his expectations.

We move closer and pick our spots for cover. This will be the hottest place in the area in a few minutes. Sgt. Krigley's plan is to have the center of our line rush the Germans with everything they have, including grenades, as Hakket and his ammo-bearer give protective fire from the other side. When the Krauts get ready to pull out as it begins to get too hot for them, they will naturally come this way. Our blocking of their exit will be another surprise for them as they try to come out the way they went in. We are not to fire until they are on the move and almost upon us. Then their only way out will be down the bare slope where we can catch them all out in the open.

I slip a bandolier from my shoulder and pull the ammunition clips out of the pockets, piling them at my right hand. I want to make sure I have enough within quick reach. Next comes my three grenades and now they lie like goose eggs in the soft dirt by my side. We can use them now if we want to. I imagine Sgt. Krigley will let us throw rocks if he thinks they will help to make his plan work.

Minutes pass like hours as we lie watching the grim scene before us. Man against man – fighting for ideals each thinks are right. How different these men might act if they met in a bar. One would invite the other to have a drink. Joking would be commonplace instead of lead and the smell of burned powder. Here we are, a few young men, out in the middle of a woods fighting to see who will kill the other in this "game" called war.

The signal for the center of our line to charge is a flurry of hand grenades from Hakket and his man. Five of the grenades hit in the center of the German's positions and explode their fury in equal directions, ripping brush and humans alike. The change of the fight pattern stuns the enemy as his firing stops for a moment and his mind goes blank. This starts a rousing cry of men's voices from our side and they rush forward throwing grenades and firing as fast as possible at the general area where the Germans are. Hakket's BAR is keeping up a steady staccato of "pom-pom-pom-pom" to pin the Krauts down. Sgt. Krigley,

Watts and I watch the action as it develops into a rout. It is as if Sgt. Krigley has written the script and the men are playing their parts to perfection. A few Germans start to move back but not wanting to go over the ridge, pull a few more with them and head our way. The rest follow and they are completely lost in their attempt to escape as our men shout and give a big show of strength. They fire continuously and hurl grenades after the fleeing enemy. As they approach the three of us, we wait with trigger fingers on the brink of firing too soon.

They are standing and running now. No more crouching and trying for cover. All they want to do is get out of the way of those firing maniacs behind them. They plunge headlong into our hidden trap and seven fall as we throw grenades and fire our semi-automatic rifles until the barrels are too hot to touch. In their pandemonium, they cannot locate us and we cut them down as if they are ten pins. Our men stop pushing forward in order to keep out of our line of fire. They have closed the door behind the fleeing men whose only way out now is down the bare slope. They turn and throw themselves over it, falling and plunging into one another as we reach the crest and pick them off one by one. None escape.

All is quiet. Our men look at each other with grim faces. We are dirty men, sweaty men, who have just lost sight of our religious teachings. We have remembered only shooting, and blood, and ripping lead that burns as it tears into a body, and killing, and knifing, and blasting and blood curdling screams that shake the very doors of heaven with their agonizing wail. We are men whose minds are at a high pitch with our bodies trembling full of hatred for the dead who lie sprawled at the bottom of the slope. The living aren't afraid of anything at this moment, and yet, in a little while, when we compose ourselves, we will all be frightened by what we have just gone through.

The sky starts to cloud up as if the Saints above who have been witnessing this orgy of killing want to shut it from their view. The thought enters my mind, "Tonight I have killed men and I have actually planned their death. How will God judge me? My only hope is His merciful forgiveness."

We move out of the area with only one casualty. He

26

has a jagged gash in his shoulder and is almost out of
his mind with pain. Watts opens the first aid pack from
his belt and sprinkles powdered sulfa on the wound. We
have no water with us so I hand the wounded man a filled
canteen from a dead German's belt to wash down some pain
killing pills.

With one man acting as a prop for the wounded man,
the patrol starts back to our bunkers with full knowledge
that we have done our part. Sgt. Krigley leads us through
the openings in the woods and traveling is much easier.
I figure we are nearing the gully that we are supposed
to stay away from according to Capt. Ronnet's orders of
last night. Suddenly two shots shatter the stillness of
the dawn.

It is light enough to see two Germans running through
the woods in the direction of their lines. It must be
the two that escaped Watts' earlier ambush and they have
come back to see if any of their men are still alive.
There aren't but they have gained their revenge as we get
to our feet and notice Hakket still on the ground, blood
flowing from his neck and shoulder. He is dead.

Sgt. Krigley lowers his head and swears softly. With
tears in his eyes, he says, "How can a man go through what
Hakket did tonight and not get a scratch - and then——?"
He swallows a choked word and appoints two men to lift
Hakket up and carry him. Watts picks up Hakket's BAR and
slings it across his shoulder. We haven't a chance to
follow the two Germans as they vanish from sight.

It is light out now and another day is here. Sgt.
Krigley radios ahead that we are coming into our lines
and the Captain is waiting for us at his bunker. He shakes
our hands and tells us to go to our bunkers and get some
sleep. Meanwhile, Sgt. Krigley proceeds to give his full
account of the night's action. We pick up our wallets,
combs, cigarettes and lighters and put them in our pockets.
I stumble down to the muddy floor of our bunker and the
torrent of questions that greets me strikes my mind with
repugnance.

"How many did you kill?"
"Any of our men killed?"
"Any close fighting?"
This questioning turns my stomach. I look down and

27

see my hands for the first time since daybreak. The red stickiness of blood covers my right hand to my wrist. Sweat stands out on my hot forehead as I remember. It is too much. I vomit on the wall, on the log floor and almost pass out. The men help me stay on my feet and after drinking my fill of cool water, I crawl into one of the sleeping holes and try to find peaceful sleep. But I can't sleep with all these memories rampaging in my brain. It is like a nightmare. I wonder if it has really happened?

"Why do civilized men have to act like barbarians? There must be another way to settle differences! There has to be---. The world cannot keep on like this much longer. Wars are getting worse and more terrible in each generation. It is always a question of military strength and secret weapons with more devastating killing power than ever before. Why?" I ask myself, "Why?" I am shaken from my thoughts by Riggins calling to me.

"What do you want?" I ask sharply.

The reply comes, "You're to report to the Captain's bunker at once."

"The Captain's bunker! What for?"

A sweet mimicing voice comes forth from Riggins, "I don't know, soldier, the Captain doesn't tell me all his plans."

Angered by this mocking, I crawl out and face the jeering voice. He has a grin on his face and I know I am just being ribbed.

"Yeah," I apologize, "I guess he doesn't."

Picking up my rifle and helmet, I stride to the Captain's bunker. My mind fills with thoughts of another patrol in daylight. I shudder and reach for a fresh pack of cigarettes. My hands tremble as I light one and the first puff fills my body with the calmness I need so badly. I think, "He wants me to get some sleep, yet he doesn't even give me a chance to relax. Something must be up. But why can't he wait until I have a few hours sleep?"

I look down at my muddy, dirty uniform and know it isn't exactly a pretty picture for the Captain's eyes. But if he wants to see me bad enough, he will have to take me as I am. "I don't give a damn!" My attitude shocks me but it still stands. "I just don't give a damn!"

Capt. Ronnet, Sgt. Krigley and Cpl. Watts are talking

and joking as I enter. They turn and greet me as I join them. A rich aroma of coffee fills the air and when I look around to locate its source, Capt. Ronnet hands me a canteen cup full and motions to a box for me to sit on. The coffee is invigorating and calms my jangled nerves. They wait for me to enjoy the coffee before telling me the business at hand.

First the Captain relates how pleased he is to learn that I can handle myself under fire, that I am a man he can depend on, and so forth and so on, until I know there will be a catch to it. I wait as Sgt. Krigley and Cpl. Watts add their comments, praising me for doing more than my share last night. "Also," the Captain adds, "we may have valuable information in our hands. The pad of paper Watts picked up by his dead Kraut looks as if it contains figures and notes. Since none of it can be deciphered by any of our men, it has been sent back to regimental headquarters."

Capt. Ronnet turns to Sgt. Krigley and asks, "Do any of your men know how to handle a BAR?"

"No, Sir," replies the Sergeant, "unless he does," motioning in my direction. I almost choke on the smoke and cough as if I really have choked

Capt. Ronnet turns to me, "How about it? Do you know how to handle a Browning Automatic Rifle?"

"No, SIR!" I reply.

"What do you mean, soldier! Every man in the United States Army has training on that piece! Isn't that right?"

I stutter and stammer, "Well, ah, Sir, when I was in basic training, a PFC sat in the middle of about two hundred of us and held up a gun and said, 'This is a BAR.' Then he put it down and worked on it for a few minutes and said, 'This is how you dismantle it.' Then he worked on it for a few minutes and held it up again and said, 'This is how you assemble it.' And that's all I know about it , Sir."

The Captain glares at me, "Have you ever fired the BAR?" His lip curls back over his teeth.

"No, Sir," I weakly answer. "In fact, I don't know a thing about the gun. You see, I was in the back row when the PFC gave us our training on it."

Cpl. Watts snickers and Sgt. Krigley has to turn his

face to keep his smile from showing. I guess it does sound like a joke to them. The Captain picks up Hakket's BAR and hands it to me, saying, "Here, you'll learn!"

We leave the bunker with me carrying the BAR that feels clumsy in my hands. Watts and Krigley assure me they will help me with it.

I ask, "What did I do to you guys to deserve this?"

Sgt. Krigley replies, "Someone has to take it and it might just as well be you."

Watts laughs.

Chapter Two

Roger is now my ammunition bearer.

We have gone through cases of regular 30 caliber shells, firing behind the lines in a ravine sheltered by dense pine trees. Armor-piercing and tracer shells have also been available and we have filled clip after clip of twenty shells each; sometimes all of one kind and then again we experiment with mixing all three in one clip. The tracer mixed with the other two makes a perfect load for night support because the tracer shells let you know if the other shells are hitting the target. We make up some extra clips of these and mark them accordingly, setting them aside as our own private stock. At the end of the day we have a large stock of clips put together and I have gained confidence in the use of the BAR.

Krigley and Watts have come to give me some tips and to watch me shoot. As we return to the bunkers, Krigley says, "The Captain wants to see you and Roger."

"Maybe he wants to give this BAR to someone who really wants it," I question.

"I doubt it," he mutters over his shoulder as he and Watts stride away from us.

Entering the command bunker, Roger and I are greeted by Capt. Ronnet as he states, "Well, Jackson, you did O.K. today on the BAR. I told Sgt. Krigley to have you come here only if he thought you could handle it."

I look over at Roger and think, "Geez, if we had done poorly today, someone else would have it. Instead we have been marked by our own conscientious attitude."

Roger looks back at me and shrugs his shoulders as if to say, "Too late now."

The Captain observes, "You've got a cleaning job ahead of you to get that barrel back in shape. You've put alot of lead through it these past three days. Take the piece completely apart and clean it with the idea that your life and others depend on its working condition." He points to an encased BAR barrel standing in the corner and says, "Put this new barrel on it and keep the old one as a spare. You, Korney, will carry it with you along with the extra clips of ammunition." Turning to me again he states, "I want you to handle this BAR all day long. Get so used to handling it that it seems like an extension of your

31

arm. Know how to take it apart and put it back together blindfolded. And do it quietly, you might have to do it some night in the dark."

"Yes, Sir," I reply. "Anything else, Sir?"

"No, not tonight. You may return to your bunker." With a quick salute, Roger and I take our leave.

A few days pass and we are told to get ready to move out. Evidently a new battalion will be moving in to replace us. We don't know where we are going but we expect heavy fighting because our unit is now filled to the man by replacements. We have had our equipment checked and worn pieces are thrown out while new ones are issued. Rumors fly rampant. Aachen, the Ardennes, Huertgen Forest, Schmidt and other destinations are mentioned.

We move out. Trucks transport us for miles to another thickly wooded pine forest where the muddy ground leaves no escape. It is knee deep in places and we wonder why anyone wants to defend it. But we are next to an important crossroad and it must be kept clear for our supply trucks.

Just before dusk we cut the lower branches off the trees and make a cross patch of them to lie on. Some of the men have straw on their branches! "Just where the hell did they get that straw?" Roger inquires contemptuously.

"Don't know," I answer, "but if I did, you can bet I'd have some."

The sound of a German liaison plane overhead quickly freezes all the men in hiding places under the trees. The pilot flies in low, just above the tree tops. You can see his helmeted head as he searches the area. "Sure hope none of the new replacements takes a pot shot at him. That's all he'd need to call in our coordinates and the incoming mail will not be enjoyed by all," Roger remarks.

"Yep, that's 'Bed Check Charlie's' job," I reply. "Call out the Kraut artillery on any suspicious sighting." After checking our area thoroughly, the liaison plane vanishes, seeking elsewhere for concealed troops, tanks or trucks.

Sleeping on the branches is not comfortable. But as tired as we are, we soon fall asleep as our bed slowly sinks in the quagmire.

The morning finds us sloshing through the mud,

32

approaching a small town. The first shots are fired at our advance scouts as they attempt to estimate the German strength and locate their gun emplacements. Our squads move forward alternately. Some are making a frontal attack, gaining cover of a stone fence, while another squad comes from the left, through the woods and out onto the open farm fields.

The crops have long been harvested and the cover is scarce. They must run a few steps and dive quickly into the mud before the enemy can get a sight on them. Some do not dive quickly enough and die in agony or cry out for a medic. The rest of the squad continues to fire and gains the line of the first houses. Our squad is in the second wave, following across the open field. The first squad is firing rapidly into the houses and thus provides us with time to move easily across the fields, firing as we advance.

I find myself squinting my eyes and tightening my jaw as I run across the open area, searching for meager cover; a plowed gully. Diving into it I can look from side to side, ascertaining my forward progress in line with the rest of the squad. Jumping up again, I zigzag toward the houses and finally reach the first squad's position. They in turn run forward, taking shelter at the corner of the second row of houses.

Now we must enter these homes and clear them of the enemy. Shots are being fired from each window. Hand grenades are freed from their firing pins and hurled through the openings. Doors are busted in and rooms sprayed with bullets. As we leave a house to move forward, we can see the enemy retreating to the center of town, firing at us and forcing us to take cover. Soon we are following them, taking house by house, as resistance stiffens. We probably have lost as many men as they have.

Now the forward battle slows to a halt as both sides regroup in the basements, gaining protective cover. I open a basement window, trying to gain a quick look outside. The action draws a hail of bullets from the basement across the street. Taking a grenade in hand, I pull the pin and pitch the explosive across the street and through the basement window. It explodes its fury sending a flash of light and a dense cloud of dust back out the window.

All is quiet and so I chance a longer look and suddenly I see an arm appear and it is heaving a potato masher grenade at my window. Quickly I close the board window and hear the grenade bounce off it and explode in the street. The noise is deafening and the concussion is sending shock waves through my ears. Roger swears quietly and holds his hands up to shield his ears but it is too late. The sound penetrates and momentarily immobilizes us.

"What the hell you doing, Jackson, starting your own war?" he exclaims, rubbing his ears to clear them. "We may be here for days. Don't rile them up any more 'till we find out where the rest of the squad is."

'O.K.," I answer, "but you better find a place where you can look out and make sure we aren't surprised by Krauts. This seems like a hot spot to me."

Sporadically for the next hour we hear random shots and explosions. I am beginning to get apprehensive not knowing where our squad is and why there hasn't been any probing shots from across the street. "Lets get out of here and find the Sarge," Roger expresses his thoughts. "We sure as hell don't want to be surrounded and attacked down here."

"I've heard a few shots and other noises, like someone running in the house on our left. Let's investigate. Dammed if I can tell German footsteps from American," I answer.

As I ascend the basement steps and push the trap door up slowly, I can peer out and see the kitchen area. To my relief there is no one there. Roger follows me across the room and out the back door. Our minds are alert and our guns are held at a ready position as we run across the back yard that recently pastured cows and a flock of chickens, their droppings making our footing precarious. Going over the wooden fence to the street, we can feel our muscles tense. Their tightening keeps us aware of our situation as we proceed at a crouch down the edge of the street.

There, ahead of us, next to the stone fence, is the rest of our squad. Sitting and lying they rest and wait for further orders. They see us coming and watch as we approach. There is no greeting as we sit next to them, comfortable in the knowledge that we have found them and for the moment are safe.

Far off in the distance we can hear the rumble of artillery as it breaks the stillness that surrounds us. Then a sharp outbreak of rifle fire punctuates the quiet, making us alert to our advanced position. Soon it passes and the hush of silence dulls our apprehension.

For the first time today I am able to look around at the area of town we are in and see it as something other than a battlefield. I wonder, "Where are the people that live in these houses? When did they leave? It had to have been yesterday by the looks of the food scraps left on the table in the kitchen and the condition of the manure in the back yards. Where did they go? Were they evacuated by truck by the German Army or did they leave of their own volition, sensing the fast approach of the Allied Army?"

The homes are sturdy and appear neat in their agelessness. Most of the furnishings are still in place as if to say, "We will wait for you to return." I remember seeing quite a few religious articles hanging on the walls and setting on end tables or buffets. Family pictures guard the seldom used parlor, while the family kitchen is the most used room, I assume.

Some houses, mainly on the edge of town, have their barns attached to the living area. Sheds are plentiful, chocked with ancient farming tools and grain storage areas are filled. Wagons and sleds are left where last used, their heavy grey wood worn to a shiny luster, hiding the strength they hold.

Beyond the stone and wooden fences are the fields we have crossed this morning. They seem so serene now, laying fallow, soaking up moisture and manure, starting the long wait for spring crops to be planted. The sun warms the roof tops, while small birds flit nervously over the smoke stained shingles, dropping quickly to the ground for a kernel of grain. Then they disappear around the corner of the barn. Snow clouds are forming in the distance but for now we are caught up in the reverie.

Capt. Ronnet strides out of the barn, zipping his pants. He calls Sgt. Krigley to assemble the squads.

Quickly we gather around the leaders and listen intently. "We are going to hold this town tonight. The

35

Germans have retreated, leaving only rear guard troops,"
reports the Captain, "and we have to dig in because they
will probably sacrifice this small town to their artillery.
Tomorrow they will surely send in some tanks. They want
that crossroad we took from them. The Sergeant will direct
the squads through the town and set up your positions on
the far side. Some of our troops are already there.
Remember, just because they retreated doesn't mean they
all left town. Some could be hiding anywhere. When you
are assigned your position, dig in and be alert. Keep
someone on guard all night. Don't screw up and depend
on someone else to do your job. It could be fatal."

"The kitchen trucks are bogged down in the mud so
you will be eating C rations until breakfast. We will
probably have a hot breakfast very early before the
artillery starts and before the tanks attempt their
penetration. The main roads are probably as bad on the
other side as they are on ours so expect them to try to
come across the farm roads. When you move out now, spread
out but don't lose sight of the rest. If there are any
Krauts still in town, they will pick off the stragglers.
Sergeant, take over."

"Yes, Sir," replies the tall heavy-set man with three
stripes on the back of his helmet.

Advancing through the deserted streets by running
short spaces and leap frogging the men ahead of us, the
squads find no resistance as we gain the outskirts. Here
we are assigned areas and again told to dig in. Roger
and I are positioned near a pile of logs in a depression
alongside a farm road where long use has created deep ruts.
"Well, let's dig our home for the night," I state flatly.
"Don't want to be unprepared for company."

The dirt is soft and easily removed from the first
two feet. Rocks make the rest of the excavation more
difficult but we are not alone as we can hear other
entrenching tools striking rocks not too far from us.

"I think it would be a good idea if we take a few
of those logs and build a protective wall behind our
foxhole, just in case some of those hiden Germans start
to fire at us from town," Roger states as he strides to
the log pile. Soon we are finished. We have logs behind
us and one in front. We also have saved the flat rocks

36

and made the floor level. A crude seat is fashioned on the dirt step that will be used for our exit. We cover the seat with grasses. It will serve as a sleeping seat for the one not on guard during the night. Poles are placed upright in the four corners and will be used to support our shelter-half if it starts to snow. We settle in and peer searchingly across the fields as night approaches.

"See anything?" Roger questions as he squints his eyes, looking for movement and listening for sounds.

"Nope," I reply, "it looks like they had enough for today. I'll take first watch. You get some sleep."

"You know what?" Roger says. "I think I'll scoop out a couple of slit trenches past the other end of that pile of logs. Might be handy to have an alternate position." Without waiting for a reply, he climbs out of the foxhole and moves down the road, past the logs and after scanning the area, chooses our fields of fire. The slit trenches will be shallow, only a foot or so deep. Just enough to protect us and long enough so we can lay down in them.

As I watch him shoveling the dirt, I think of how long we have been together. Just a short time and yet we have become veterans. We can depend on each other. Roger is a medium built young man. A farm boy who can cope with adversity, hard work, and doesn't complain about our living conditions. His light brown hair is wavy under his helmet and his bushy eye brows give his face a heavy look, deep and thoughtful. Large hands grab the shovel with strength and the dirt flies in the air as he places it around the trenches.

The sky is dark with snow clouds lumbering heavily over us. A sharp drop in the temperature informs us of the oncoming storm and we shiver as we finish stretching our shelter-halves over the supporting corner poles. The wind is gusty and by the time Roger is asleep on the step, wrapped in his blanket, the snow flakes start to swirl around us.

The quiet scene before me is peaceful. I think of the many times I have stood guard, my eyes alert, my thoughts filled with dreams of home. Nothing breaks the deep silence and my watch passes. I now can sleep while Roger stands guard. It feels good to sit down and wrap up in a blanket. The outside air is colder now and the protection of the dirt walls prevents the wind from piercing my jacket. Falling asleep is easy. In two hours Roger will wake me as we take turns on guard duty.

The night passes this way until early in the morning. As I look out over the snow covered fields, I hear the faint rush of air, then the whistle grows louder as an artillery shell screams over our foxhole. It bursts fifty yards to our rear, exploding with a shower of dirt and snow. Roger jumps up quickly, throwing the blanket from his shoulder. "Damm," he says, "here is the artillery and we haven't had breakfast yet!"

More bursts of artillery are landing in our company area, exploding death in every direction. I stand waiting for the first German to show his head from the cover in which he is hiding. Soon they will come, charging toward me, all care abandoned as they step into our line of fire. The thought of again shooting at another human being gives me a fright that is larger than the shells whistling overhead.

Here they come, running over the low hill shouting and brandishing rifles. The small arms firing is starting and soon the heat of this battle will be as fierce as the rest. Shells burst over our machine gun emplacements knocking them out. This leaves me with the only automatic weapon.

A German tank rumbles from the patch of woods to the left and begins firing as it zeros in on us. The first shell lands close to our foxhole and the second a little closer. Our experience of past battles comes to our rescue and we climb from the foxhole with our extra ammo, zigzagging to the slit trenches as the hole we have just vacated blows up with a heaving motion. Dirt falls around me as I slide into my new trench. Roger is right beside me, hugging the ground.

The Bazooka team has loaded and fires a rocket into the pride of the Panzer division. The tank is hit and is silent, another relic to dot the raging landscape. The enemy is everywhere before me and aiming is hardly necessary. It doesn't seem right. They are running out in the open and we are huddled in slit trenches and foxholes protecting our bodies from their bullets. Our artillery is probing theirs and also finding the range to clear the area in front of us.

"There," I point out to Roger. "There in the woods at the right. Four more tanks. Damn! We don't need them to zero in on us." The tanks are firing as they approach, their 88's booming in the staccato of the rifle fire.

Roger is firing his M-1 rhythmically, stopping only to supply me with more clips for the BAR. Geysers of dirty snow spout in front of us as the approaching Germans attempt to cover their forward rushes. We are protected from their direct fire. Now the tanks are flanking us and firing their machine guns up and down our positions.

"We need a deep hole," Roger screams trying to be heard over the incessant noise of the battle.

"Then let's get back to our foxhole. It's alot deeper now," I holler back to him. Both of us grab supplies of ammunition. Roger slings the extra BAR barrel over his shoulder and we run behind the log pile and slide down into the excavation that last night was our foxhole. The bullets are singing over us now as our movement has caught the attention of the attackers.

Swiftly I open the musette bag that contains grenades. A quick look over the rim of our hole confirms my suspicions. They are coming directly at us. Without hesitation Roger and I pull pins from the explosives and hurl them into the rushing masses. The deafening sound stops them momentarily as we pitch four more grenades at them. Their supporting tanks are providing enfilading fire with fierce bursts that tear at the dirt around us. We cannot raise our heads.

Suddenly our artillery begins to rake the area, pounding relentlessly, flushing the tanks from their positions and demoralizing the troops crossing the open fields. Roger steals a glance from our hole and screams, "They're retreating! We've stopped them!"

"Well, let's stop more of them," I yell through the cacophony of sound. "Give me some armor-piercing. I'd like to give those tanks some of their own music."

Sliding in the clip and resting the BAR on its bipod, I relax and fire a steady stream into the lead tank's broadside. I believe some of the pellets pierce the thinner back armor and ricochet around inside, killing the tank's crew. Roger shouts, "You got 'em, Bob.! They're a dead duck! Try for another," he yells gleefully. However, it was the bazooka team who had stopped the tank.

An anti-tank gun fires from behind us, its roar a pain to our ears. Another tank is stopped.

With part of our artillery searching out the tanks, plus our rifle grenade and bazooka teams running after the retreating metal monsters, there is no need for me to direct my fire on those targets. I concentrate on the disappearing troops. They are running back to the woods, leaving their dead and wounded, sentencing them to the formidable ordeal of earth shaking explosions as our big guns trail them pitilessly. I realize that I am soaked with perspiration as the cold winter wind sends a shiver through me. But we are alive. Alive to fight again.

"Some of the guys didn't make it," Roger avers quietly, looking over our company area.

"Here comes the Captain," I call to his attention.

Both of us stare rigidly at the officer as he speaks. "Korney, you're on the chow detail. The kitchen trucks are just behind that first row of houses. Help them bring breakfast up to these men." He leaves as quickly as he came, continuing his inspection of the company. Roger shoulders his M-1 and runs to the rear, his smile as large as his appetite.

Medics are attending the wounded, placing them on stretchers and removing them to the ambulances that have made their way through the muddy roads. Quickly the ambulances start their return trip, churning up the mud again, carrying their precious contents hopefully to safety. When the medics finish with the wounded, they turn to the dead, placing them in body bags, and carefully load them into the back of a half track that is traversing the area. Soon they are gone.

I am deep in thought, looking out over the open fields that are heavily dotted with dead or wounded Germans. Their medics have exited the woods and with large red and white jackets on, they proceed to attend their afflicted comrades. I cannot bear the sight behind me and I don't care to watch the one in front of me. I can only slide to the bottom of the muddy hole I am in and thank God that he has spared me.

After a short time, I am able to compose my thoughts

and light a cigarette. Others are doing the same. I can
see them solemnly looking from their foxholes, puffing
slowly, letting the nicotine quiet their nerves.

The sound of footsteps approaching breaks into my
vacuum of thoughts and I glance around to see Roger coming
with two mess kits piled high with food steaming in the
cold air. Canteen cups of hot coffee are set down beside
the pile of logs and I join him. I am ravenous. The food
smells delicious. Pancakes smothered in butter and maple
syrup. Slices of ham, hot and juicy cover two fried eggs.
Large pieces of buttered bread, toasted lightly, fill the
mess kit and I lose no time tasting its contents. The
hot coffee warms me inside. I look over at Roger as he
is devouring his food. He senses my movement and looks
up. We only have to have our eyes meet for a minute to
commend each other on our supportive action in battle.
Now we can rest.

Again we are being replaced. The last week has been
spent in our new foxhole alongside the old one. The Germans
have shelled our area intermittently and we repulsed their
one feeble attack. Now the orders are, "Prepare to move
out."

As the new men come to substitute for us, we join
our company by the kitchen trucks. Rations are issued
and we are marched in loose formation through the town.
It is mid-morning and the sun is warm though snow remains
on the ground. Houses are gutted and walls knocked down,
exposing the interiors where just a few weeks ago people
lived. Smoldering ruins of barns and sheds, houses and
trees, fill the air with an acrid smell. Roads are blocked
by the ruins and we must crawl over the debris. Yards
are littered with pieces of furniture torn apart by the
German artillery. Lace curtains droop grotesquely from
shattered window frames while doors slantingly hang on
one hinge. Twisted farm machinery lie in abstract form.
It is total destruction. We leave it behind.

Rumors are the 28th is going back to Paris for R and
R!

The men are happy as we reach the line of trucks
waiting for us. We clamber aboard them amid incessant
talking. Muddy G I shoes stomp on the bed of the truck
and singing breaks out. Laughter fills us with relaxation

41

as we watch the thick forests slip behind us and we emerge to open farm country and better roads.

The next day we are quartered in a large village, Diekirch, next to a railroad track where we will wait for our train. The peaceful countryside and the serenity of undisturbed thoughts let us wallow in our happiness. By squads we are called to take showers and wash our clothes at the local school. Hot meals are served from the kitchen units. Letters are written with care not to tell too much of the severity of our recent battles. We are healthy, clean and amply fed. This will please worried minds at home. Scenes of men shaving, getting hair cuts, sewing up a tear in their pants, cleaning rifles, water proofing their G I shoes, and reading the just arrived mail seems so far removed from the war. For the moment we are content.

After the third day, we are getting restless. Our train has not come to transport us to Paris. Some of the men have left the bivouac area and searched out local taverns against orders. There are reports of brawls taking place after a few drinks as these muscular fighting men seek an outlet for their pent up energy. The people of the village have kept to the interior of their dwellings, frightened by the tension that is building, afraid of these men who have liberated them from the yoke of the Nazi Army and its cruel regime. They wish to celebrate the possibility of a new freedom, however, they are restrained by their fear. We are called to formation and roll calls are taken to ascertain who is absent. Friends answer for the absentees and nothing is gained.

The dreaded word comes. Our train will be delayed for a lengthy period and therefore we are ordered to pack up and prepare to move out. Two days later we find ourselves digging foxholes and patrolling on the front lines near the Luxembourg, Belgium and German borders. There is no sign of either side trying to gain on the other and in fact, the lines are a few miles apart. Our patrols are sent out in daylight across open fields, over rolling hills that slope down on the other side to the Our River. We are ordered to patrol up and down the river to certain points and to go no further.

Comfortable knowing that within a couple of weeks our train will come for us, we relax and enjoy the cool

December weather. We prepare our fox holes and guard a country road that is bisected by a narrow bridge over a small recessed stream. Secure in the protective covering of a fringe of leafless trees, we can see beyond the sunken road, the bridge and the fields, to the crest of the hills a mile away. Our platoon of forty-five men form a right angle position at the curve in the road about fifty yards from the bridge. My position is at the vertex of the right angle.

It does not dawn on us that we only carry basic quantities of ammunition and two days rations. There are no other companies on either side of us for hundreds of yards and no effort has been made to establish radio communications to our left, right or to the rear. The kitchen unit has been set up in a deserted farm house one hundred yards to our left and we stroll over there to eat as our squads are notified. Behind us a wooded hill gently slopes upward for fifty yards then gradually levels off and recedes into the distant non-descript prairie and wooded patches. There is no war activity to make us feel threatened. It is only a week until Christmas.

I'm to go on patrol duty tonight. Just another routine reconnaissance to the river. We will post on a hillside overlooking its banks for a couple of hours, then scout both up and down the river to the prescribed limits and return to our platoon position by midnight.

The squad is formed and with Cpl. Watts as the leader, we openly walk across the narrow bridge and step onto the frozen grasses of the level field. There is no attempt to conceal our movements. While we do not talk or make any unnecessary noises, there is no stealth in our approach and we arrive at the wooded crest of the hill. The Our River is rushing below us in its never ending race to locate the sea. We find a brushy hillside and conceal ourselves behind stumps, bushes and hummocks, observing the far side of the river.

The coolness in the air is sharper than it was earlier and soon our bodies are stiff and cramped. The sky is clear and stars light the darkness, giving us the ability to plainly see across on the German side. We wait. At quarter to ten Cpl. Watts splits the squad, leaving half to observe from our position and taking the rest of the

43

men with him to scout the river. Roger and I remain to observe. By ten-thirty they return and Watts gathers our half of the squad to patrol down the river.

It is good to be able to stretch our legs and soon the warmth of movement relieves the cold that had penetrated our stiff bodies. Following a path that winds just below the crest of the hill, we can see the river and the spirals of fog that are starting to form as the cold air touches the warmer earth and water. Cpl. Watts is moving faster than usual and we reach our down river destination quicker than planned. Without hesitation Watts continues on, scouting out new territory along the river.

We have progressed a mile into new fields and wooded hillsides along the river. Suddenly Watts holds his hand up to stop the patrol. He signals for silence as he turns his head, listening intently. All of us turn our ears in the direction he is pointing and we can hear strange poundings and motors running in the distance. Slipping quickly into the protective brush, we move forward to gain a view of the riverside activity.

Fog is covering the far side of the river where motors are idling but in the middle of the stream, men are working on a submerged bridge. It is six inches below the water and the muffled sounds of their construction now reach our ears clearly. The straining sound of a motor reveals a truck loaded with timbers emerging from the fog as it delivers its contents across the bridge. There is a rush of men to unload it and guide the timbers into position, anchoring them to form the final ramp.

We are awed by the possible consequences of our discovery. This bridge must have taken two weeks to construct, yet it is hidden from view by the water rushing over its top. Surely it must have been built only at night, safe from the view of our liaison planes. We have discovered an important covert enemy activity and Watts leads us away in haste. Double timing it back to the rest of the squad, we are given no break as our leader tells them to return with us to our platoon area.

Following Cpl. Watts to the officers' post, Roger and I listen breathlessly as he reports on our patrol's discovery. Capt. Ronnet and 2nd Lt. Cummings listen attentively. When the report is complete and there are no questions, the Captain states, "Good job, men. We'll have demolition teams blow it up and bomb it. Lieutenant, send a messenger back to battalion in the morning informing them of this new development."

We are dismissed. Roger and I cannot understand why this isn't being reported at once to battalion headquarters. What is the reason for no radio communication between units? The fog closes in, blanketing the entire sector. A few hours of sleep in our foxhole will be welcomed but sleep does not come. "Roger, what do you think about the bridge?" I question.

"Don't know, Bob," he replies, "but it sure is stout. Reckon it would hold tanks and trucks. They sure as hell didn't build it for us so they must be planning on coming across the river soon. Don't like the looks of it."

"I don't like the situation it puts us in! We don't have communications, rations, ammo, tank support or even an idea where our flanking units are. If they come across that bridge, then they will surely head for this bridge in front of us. We have only forty-five men to stop them. A couple of machine guns with no mortars and only basic ammo supplies is no way to stop a big push. I can't understand why that bridge wasn't spotted weeks ago and blown up?"

"Well, at least it was found tonight," Roger replies.

"Yeah," I answer, "maybe it wasn't supposed to be discovered. Hell, the whole German army could cross over it tonight."

"Let's get some sleep, Bob. I'm tired," Roger yawns.

We are awakened from a deep sleep just before dawn by an artillery bombardment that is saturating the area. The booming explosions rock the earth and shower us with dirt. Our ears are hurting from the deafening sound and the concussion gives us a headache. The fog has not lifted and we cannot see what is going on even within our platoon area. Swirls of mist dance away from the explosions and are then sucked back into the vacuum. We crouch down in our foxhole and pray for the pounding to cease. It doesn't.

After an hour we discern a slight let up but it does not stop. The constant probing of the area has mesmerized us and we can almost detect a rhythmic beat to its incessant reoccurrence. One thing we have detected: our artillery is silent. We have not been able to hear one answering round.

It is almost noon when the throbbing noise stops. The fog has lifted and the landscape around us reaching as far as we can see, has changed. The pock-marked field that leads to the crest of the hill beside the river has changed to look like a flat of dominoes. And there on the crest is a line of tanks. Huge monsters. They and the men that swarm about them are out of our range, over a mile away. They wait. We can hear their engines rumbling in unison as they idle. Their 88's are pointing directly at us. We wait.

My mouth is dry. Looking at the formidable condition we face has drained my senses. Taking a drink of water from my canteen and feeling its cold presence as I gulp it down, helps me to regain my thoughts. Our pitiable cover of trees has almost been decimated. I can see Capt. Ronnet and 2nd Lt. Cummings attempting to salvage our machine guns that have been knocked out. Roger and I are the front corner of the company's position, or what's left of it. The right angle of foxholes spreads out to each side of us. There are gaps in the line. Instead of foxholes, there are smoking craters where men have died. The smell of explosives permeate the air. We note that neither the road nor the bridge we are guarding have been hit. It's plain that a big push is in effect and we will not escape the brunt of it. They will force their way down the road and cross the bridge only fifty yards in front of us. We have no way to stop them.

Roger opens a can of beans from our C rations and hands it to me. We do not speak. There is no need for words. We can only wait for orders. Capt. Ronnet openly walks over to our foxhole and informs me that my BAR is the only automatic bit of firepower left in the platoon. "Korney," the Captain orders, "go over to the 30 caliber machine gun position and bring a case of ammo to your foxhole. You will have to keep clips filled for Jackson's BAR." Turning to me he continues, "I'm going to have to ration ammo to the other men. You keep that BAR going as long as it will still fire. Let them think we are knee deep in ammo. We have five rifle grenades and that's all. We will try to stop the lead tank on the bridge to block the road. We've lost our bazooka team. Can't locate the bazooka. Both the 50 caliber and 30 caliber pieces are beyond use. You better conserve your water and rations as the kitchen unit was destroyed first thing this morning."

"Sir," I ask, "how many men do we have left?"

He looks me square in the eye, his jaw is firmly set. Quietly he replies, "Thirty-two, including Cummings and myself."

"Any chance of replacements?" I ask, already suspecting the answer.

"No chance at all," he states firmly then adds, "and we do not have communications to call for any. Our orders are to hold this area." His head is bowed now. It is difficult for him to keep the stern firmness in his voice. He is squatting down, sitting on his heels at the edge of our foxhole. Reaching out he grabs a handful of dirt and slowly lets it run through his fingers. I watch the dirt sifting down and when it is all gone I realize the finality of his words. "Sgt. Krigley and Cpl. Watts are both dead. They tried to move the fifty caliber gun and were caught out in the open."

Again he picks up a handful of dirt and gradually lets it sift through. Then rising quickly and brushing his hands off on his pants he strides on, making his final check on the remnants of his command. The tank motors rumble in the background, reminding us of our plight.

Roger returns with the case of ammunition. His face is drawn. The ever-ready smile has left. "It's a mess over there," he says quietly. "They didn't have a prayer of a chance. Damn, I hate to see all these good men wasted."

"Only thirty-two of us left," I reply, "including the Captain and Lieutenant." I pause, then looking out over the road and bridge, I inform Roger that we are ordered to hold our position.

"What the hell for," he replies. It's not a question, just a flat statement that describes the futility of it all.

The afternoon is passing and we hope that dusk will arrive before the onslaught starts. I know that our orders are to hold but I can't help but express my feelings. "Maybe they won't attack today and tonight we can pull out of this hopeless position."

I can hear the far off raging battle and by its sound I can tell that on both sides of us, our lines have been pushed back or at least penetrated. We are left out here alone, trying to hold a section of road that we know they can take from us any time they want . "Why the hell weren't we pulled back with our flanking units so at least there would be some semblance of a cohesive unit? Now they can go around us and get behind our lines easily."

Roger replies flatly again, "Around us or through us."

"Yeah, guess you're right," I utter in matter-of-fact tone. "We can never stop 'em."

Waiting for the day to end or the attack to begin is becoming painfully tiring. Our tense muscles want to relax. Taking off my glasses I wipe the film of dust from them. My eyes are sore from straining them all day. Gripping the BAR in readiness has almost paralyzed my fingers. Shoulders that ache find soothing comfort as I rotate my arms. Flexing my muscles seems to relax them and bending my knees gives my legs a feeling of relief. I wonder in anxiety what will become of us. "Is this our final battle? Should I write a letter and maybe have it found on my body and sent home with my personal belongings? Will our army stiffen and attack quickly, relieving us from our orders to hold this isolated bridge? Will our ammo hold out? Our rations? Our water?" Roger is filling clips for the BAR. I can read his thoughts. They are the same as mine.

Dusk is approaching. The air is turning colder. We can hear faint sounds of activity from some of the other foxholes. Then there is silence, except for the idling motors of the tanks upon the crest of the hill. We wait.

Night comes quickly. Roger stands guard as I fall asleep wrapped in my blanket, holding a hard C ration biscuit in my cold hand. During the night Roger and I relieve each other at guard duty. The fog is thick, right down to the ground, limiting our watchfulness. Our ears must be our eyes. The cold dampness of the foxholes seep through our clothing, making shivers course up and down our tired bodies. Just before dawn I wake Roger so we can have time for a bite to eat. A few crackers with potted meat, cold water and a cigarette complete our breakfast.

Something alerts us as we both stop in mid motion to listen. There is the noise again. It's a swishing sound and it seems as though it is not more than thirty feet in front of us. Stealthily we take our position at the rim of the foxhole, Roger with his M-1 and grenades while I settle the BAR against my shoulder, placing extra clips next to my right hand. The noise has stopped in front of us. Off to the left we hear another swishing noise, then again in front of us. Now to the right. I tap Roger's shoulder and when he glances over, I point to my left ear and then to the three areas where the noises came from.

Roger nods his head in understanding. He shifts his position, facing a little more to the left while I center myself on his right. Reaching into the musette bag, I quietly take out a hand grenade and lay it like an egg in the soft dirt in front of me. Then I take out two more and place them alongside the first.

The noise has stopped again. We listen carefully. Roger glances behind us and listens. Nothing. The furtive movements seem to be retreating from us.

Then, like a curtain, the fog rises up three feet from the ground. There is still a faint haze but we can plainly see eight German soldiers hugging the ground. Their fog cover has vanished. They have been creeping up on our position and soon would have been in our foxholes. A grenade bursts among them. The other men have also seen them and two more grenades are hurled at their retreat as they run for the safety of the sunken road. Two of them are hit and now the air is filled with their screams. We can see more German helmets peeking over the banks of the road. An arm raises and throws a grenade at our position. It's a concussion grenade and it bursts with alarming noise, ringing in our ears, momentarily halting our action.

The wounded Germans are crying out for help. Neither side seems to want to start the action again. No shots are fired. Minutes pass. We can hear the German in charge yelling out orders, directing his troops dispersal. We can only get a glimpse of them as they move in a crouch, spreading out along the road.

Capt. Ronnet yells to his men in the end foxhole, "If they start going past you on the road, give them a couple of grenades to stop them. Don't let them get around you."

The German officer's voice is controlled as he calmly calls for medics to stand up. Holding a white flag, they near their wounded comrades only fifty feet from us. No one speaks. No shots are fired. All eyes are on the drama of saving the men. The medics quickly examine the wounds and call out to their officer. Another white flag is raised and two men with stretchers run to assist the medics. Soon the stretchers are loaded and they disappear across the bridge.

A new sound is heard far up on the road. A German tank is coming. We can now see its vague form in the fog that surrounds it. Lt. Cummings shouts from our right, "Rifle grenade team, hold your fire until it gets on the bridge."

The roar of the tank's motor holds our attention. The behemoth's cleats churn up the dirt road, throwing chunks of dirt into the air behind it. The fog is still only four feet off the ground and so the tank crew is partially blinded by its density. We can see it clearly from our lower position. The hatch is closed and the barrel of the menacing 88 is rotating from side to side. The machine gun ports are open. A huge swastika emblazons its side. There are more soldiers trotting behind it. We can only watch its approach. We must depend on the rifle grenades to stop it. I have no armor-piercing clips with me as they were left with the supply trucks when we waited for our train. All we have is a basic supply, twenty clips of regular shells, plus the case from the machine gun emplacement and a musette bag filled with grenades.

The tank is twenty feet from the bridge when the rifle grenade team fires their first round. It hits the front armor at an angle and explodes its fury without penetrating. The Germans along the road sense the urgency of this attack and small arms fire breaks out. We answer it with rifle fire up and down our lines. The BAR speaks out its rhythm as the Germans duck behind the road bank. The tank is now entering the narrow bridge, its 88 spouting lethal war heads and its machine guns raging at the feeble attempt to stop it.

Once again the rifle grenade is fired, this time at

the broadside and it penetrates, ricocheting around the interior searching out the crew and killing them. The driver in his last throes of life has turned his tank sideways and it wedges tightly between the two sides of the bridge, racing its motor and squirming tighter and tighter until it can move no more. The rear end of the tank is facing us and the bridge is neatly blocked. Smoke pours out of the engine ventilators and as quickly as it is seen, the Germans are running back toward their crest of the hill position. They don't want to be anywhere around the tank if it burns and the fuel ignites the ammunition. If it does explode, we will be near a fireworks display that will be awesome.

There are no German soldiers on the road in front of us. They have all left and we can only watch the hulking tank emit smoke. It is only mid-morning and the fog has finally lifted. The sun's warmth is welcome and we crouch in our foxhole puffing on cigarettes, one eye on the far hill and one eye on the tank. Again we wait.

Roger has set up a can of sterno and after lighting it, places his canteen cup full of water on it. Soon we will have coffee. The thought calms us. We can hear voices from the foxholes on both sides of us. Silence is no longer needed and the sound of voices is reassuring. I find myself taking inventory of the ammo. We used up over half a case plus the original twenty clips. I can't seem to account in my mind the action that would call for so much expenditure of ammo. We have four grenades left.

Capt. Ronnet slithers through the mud and reaches our foxhole. "How's the ammo supply?" he questions.

"Not quite half a case left, Sir," I answer.

"Grenades?"

"Four, Sir."

"Huh," he grunts, "some of the men are completely out." He pauses to analyze the problem. "Fill twelve clips and then have Korney pass one half of what's left to the men on either side of you. Tell them to fill no more than five clips each for their M-1's and pass it on." He moves toward the right line of foxholes, stopping at each one for a word. Then he disappears to the rear.

"Twelve clips, hell," I spit out in anger. "What good are just twelve clips?"

51

Roger is silent as he fills the twelve for the BAR and then fills five for his M-1.

"I'll be back," he says as he drags a supply of shells to the foxhole on our right. Within minutes he is back and drags a supply to the left. "Just like Santa Claus," he jokes as he slides back in our hole, "bringing presents to all the good ol' boys."

The coffee is ready; its aroma tantalizing me. Roger pours half of the coffee into my canteen cup and we both sip gingerly on our hot beverage. It warms our insides and the feeling of anxiety melts into oblivion.

New feelings arise. Holding the warming cup in my hands, I ask Roger, "We better make up our minds as to what we're going to do when we run out of ammo."

"Yeah," he answers, "we sure don't have many alternatives."

"Who knows, maybe they'll send us supplies tonight, although I doubt it."

"Naw, they won't. Hell, I doubt if battalion even knows we're here."

"Or cares."

The finality of my last statement seems to say it all. No further words are needed on the subject. But there are thoughts flooding my brain. "Just what will we do when we run out of ammunition? Does anybody really know about our predicament? Why were we positioned out here in the first place? It's almost like being a decoy! Surely the Germans have by-passed us and have punched a huge hole in our lines. I wonder how deep the bulge goes? Are our strategists letting them expend their last ordinances, giving them room for their last gasp and they don't want it stopped way up here? Is our platoon really expendable? I wonder how many more companies are being thrown out as bait, with just enough supplies to harass the enemy without him getting suspicious?" My original thought comes back to me. "What will happen when we run out of ammo? I don't know the answer! I just don't know the answer. Maybe we won't even live long enough to have to make a decision."

The coffee is gone. The cup has turned cold in my hands. Waiting for another day to pass seems to be an ineffectual way to fight a war. No use going on patrol. We know right where the enemy is and what he is doing.

52

And also what he is about to do. We just don't know what we are going to do. The afternoon passes without incident. We take turns standing up, looking out from the foxhole, watching the far hillside. We can see movement there but nothing more threatening than the presence of the Germans.

Late in the day, while I'm heating water for coffee and opening the last two containers of K rations, Roger swears softly, "Damn. Here they come."

Quickly I stand up and survey the field before us. It's true. Hundreds of soldiers are coming toward us. They start to fire their rifles from half a mile away. Roger answers them with a few rounds. Other foxholes are also firing and I can see men dropping in the field. It is hard to restrain myself. I want to support our firepower and yet I know I must conserve the precious few clips I have.

As the charging German lines approach and break into a run, zigzagging and diving to the ground only to get up and come forward again, firing their rifles to keep us pinned down, I open fire with the BAR. Rotating it from left to right I can see its effect as the targets stagger and fall, not rising again. The attack is only two hundred yards from us and they keep running forward regardless of their losses. We can hear their bullets singing over our positions and digging up the dirt around us. I know some of our men are hit and there is no medic to assist them.

Capt. Ronnet crawls to our foxhole and points to the right. The Germans are flanking us and he wants me to concentrate my firepower on this new danger. Changing my position, I pour an enfilading stream of lead into their movement. They stop momentarily, finding themselves discovered. They hit the ground, answering my attack furiously. Capt. Ronnet is caught in the return fire and now lies dead just behind us.

In order to stop the flanking movement and also escape the hail of bullets from their position, I must get below the rim of the foxhole and then jump up, quickly firing as I rise, pinning them down in turn. Then as I drop down again they rise up and fire. This is using up our ammo too fast and I realize I must change the pace of the action. Firing quickly, I duck down into the foxhole and without stopping, rise again, surprising them as they rise to fire. They are caught in the burst from the BAR and several are hit. The rest retreat to their frontal line.

Turning my attention to the road and bridge, I notice the attack has stalled. Helmets appear over the road bank, peering out but providing a small target. Roger hurls a grenade and the helmets disappear. He throws a second grenade and the helmets move up the road ducking down to the stream under the bridge and continue out of sight. Rifle fire has slackened and only sporadic shots are heard from the foxholes. The attack has been stopped and we have used up about all of our ammunition. I find I have my last clip in the BAR and it is almost expended. We have one grenade left.

"How many clips you got left?" I ask Roger.

He shakes his head and answers, "None."

"Isn't this a hell of a mess?" I question. "No ammo, no food, no nothing! Not even an officer or non-com left! Hell, I don't have any idea how many men are left in the foxholes."

"Yeah," Roger adds, "we sure can't fight our way out of this without men and ammo."

Silence surrounds us as we contemplate our alternatives. Staring into the dusk of evening, the cold snow glinting like scattered diamonds in the last rays of the sun, we find only confused thoughts that give us no escape. "We have been ordered to hold this position. That we have done but to what avail? We can hold it no longer. We do not have the means to do so. What is left but death, retreat or surrender? Which will be the answer? We can't walk away from our positions because we don't know where to go. What has become of our army? Where is sanctuary? Is all lost? How many of us are left out of our decimated platoon? How many? Who is to take charge of the remnants?" The questions keep repeating as the night grows dark and cold. We shiver and only part of it is from the temperature. We realize the war is over for us. We will face our future in the morning.

Following the rules of war, we decide to take turns on guard duty again tonight. The silence is overwhelming, leading our thoughts to death or capitulation. I am hungry, thirsty and cold. Standing at the edge of the foxhole,

54

with the BAR propped up against the dirt wall, I wait for the first rays of the warming sun to bring about the new day.

It comes on quickly. The scene before us today is the same, with activity on the crest of the hill in front of the tanks. "What are they waiting for?" Roger asks quietly. "Why don't they just come and get it over with?"

"I don't know," I find myself answering in soft tones. "Maybe this isn't such an important bridge or road as we were made to believe. Maybe our mission is finished and the Krauts will just mop us up as a routine exercise. Surely they know we are low on ammo and men. Damn, I wish I knew what is expected of us."

"Let's ask the Captain. He can give us about as much information as we've been able to come up with." Roger states grimly.

"You got any military information on you that you don't want the Germans to find?" I ask.

"No," is the answer.

"Me neither, but maybe the Captain does. Search him and we'll destroy anything that is not personal property."

Roger crawls out of the foxhole and rolls the Captain over. "Geez," I hear Roger mutter as he looks at the Captain's face. Quickly he empties the pockets and tosses a map and a note pad to me. Then he rejoins me in our hole.

"Can't make head or tail out of any of this," I mutter to Roger. "But I'll bet the German intelligence could. Let's burn them now!" The small fire of paper burns brightly for a moment and then is gone. Little heat is felt by our chilled hands.

A noise to our left signals activity and we both peer over the rim of the foxhole. "There, see them," I whisper. "That's our men standing out there with their hands up."

"Yeah," Roger whispers breathlessly. "They must have surrendered."

"Listen!" I order. "Listen! They are giving up in the foxhole next to us."

The air is filled with emotion. We can see two more men join the group with their hands in the air. "We're next," I whisper. I lay the BAR against the edge of the foxhole and jump against the stock, breaking it, leaving it a useless weapon.

"They're coming," Roger whispers in terror.

"There's more of them coming from behind us too," I add.

Thinking of Jean and home, instantly reminds me to slip Jean's class ring off of my finger and hide it in my shoe. I glance at the white mark it has left on my finger and quickly rub dirt on the area, hiding its existence from view. Roger is climbing out of the foxhole, raising his hands in surrender.

"Raus! Raus!" the German soldiers shout at me, aiming their rifles with trigger fingers ready to fire into me at the least sign of resistance. They hurry us to join the other prisoners standing in a line on the open ground above the road.

"My God. There are so few. Only eighteen of us have survived!"

We are lined up in a rank facing the fifty or so enemy who are leveling their guns at us. As we see them now, we wonder how long the war will last. They are old men and young boys, some not older than fourteen or fifteen, with kitchen pots on their heads for helmets! Only three in this group seem to be regular army and they are in their twenties. They immediately begin to search us, stripping us of watches, rings, money, cigarettes, lighters, knives, papers and identification. The guard searching me has taken all of my possessions and is now rifling through my wallet. He holds up a picture of Jean and questions, "Frau?"

"Yes," I mutter. Next is a picture of my mother and three brothers. He only nods his head and returns my empty wallet, the two pictures and my comb to my back pocket. Then checking my shirt pocket, he finds my rosary. Looking at the crucifix, he pauses for an instant, then quickly says, "Gut." He lets the string of precious beads slide slowly through his fingers back into my shirt pocket. He and I are staring at each other eye to eye, for the first time searching out the thoughts that fill our minds. There is no common ground, no recognition, only one soldier with power over the other. He does not search my shoes. The ring is safe. He moves on to search Roger who is standing beside me.

My concentration, while standing with my hands in

the air, is on a machine gun team setting up their weapon in front of us. Methodically they place the tripod and connect it to the piece. I guess that it is comparable to our 30 caliber. A box of ammunition is placed alongside it with the top open revealing the belt that is quickly fed into the chamber. With a measured hand motion the bolt is cocked and the area in front of and widely to each side of the gun is cleared of Germans.

The gunner is seated on the ground with his legs wide spread, his hands on the grips. With a leer on his face, he aims at our midsection, leveling the barrel up and down our rank, measuring us for distance within his field of fire. I stare at the machine gun. Some of the German soldiers have relaxed and stand at ease off to one side. I can only think of the sight we had seen before where American prisoners had been lined up against a stone wall and massacred by the Germans, leaving their bodies to be found by the Americans as they retook the area. The horror at the time was incomprehensible and now we are faced with the reality of a similar fate.

I am brought to a state of fear as my steel helmet is removed from my head and the plastic liner is handed back to me. Glancing up and down our rank, I see others replacing the helmet liner to their head. The search is almost over. Some of the men have dropped their hands to their side after replacing their head gear and are sharply told to raise their hands again. They do as they are ordered as the sun begins to hide itself behind a cloud, taking away its meager warmth and letting a chill creep over us.

The search is ended and the searchers back off behind the machine gun. It is still leveled at us, rotating from side to side, its black opening poised to spew death. There is no sound as we stand there stiffly, our faces tense, our bodies suddenly exuding sweat that trickles down the center of our backs. Our stomachs are sucked in waiting for the onslaught of the hot lead, finding no way to relax. Breathing is in short gasps drawn between clenched teeth and released through a runny nose. Fists are made high in the air as we stand there wavering, our strength slowly being drained as the moment arrives.

A short burst from the machine gun makes us crouch

as the lead passes over our heads. The guards laugh as they now come forward and lead us to the edge of the road and force us to jump down the short embankment. We are marched toward the narrow bridge, passing bloody spots along the road where men were wounded or killed. I am almost in shock as I'm sure the other prisoners are. We have survived our first cruel moments of surrender.

The tank on the bridge is being pulled clear. There is room for us to pass and we march surrounded by guards across the shell pocked field toward the hill crest. As we reach the top I turn and look back. German tanks and soldiers are passing by our empty foxholes. The scene disappears as we are led down to the river and across the underwater bridge we had discovered three nights ago. Our feet are soaked as we plod through the water. Reaching the far side we continue up a muddy road.

I think, "What lies ahead of us?" The enormity of it all dawns on me. I realize we are prisoners of war!

Chapter Three

The small barn is cold, no longer heated by the bodies of the cows that have been taken away. We shiver in its penetrating air. The door is locked and the one window is boarded up. A sparse floor cover of straw barely shields us from the cold dampness of manure. We are too tired to stand after marching continuously for twenty-four hours and so we sit on the pungent floor not able to sleep. We think despondently of our condition.

"I'm hungry," Roger grumbles, "and a drink of water would also be welcome. Wouldn't you think they would give us something to eat and drink?"

"Maybe they will at breakfast time," I answer.

"Well, hell, it's breakfast time and more already!" he exclaims in exasperation.

"Then I guess we miss breakfast. Let's start thinking of dinner," I laugh indulging in a bit of teasing.

Roger looks at me and then looks away. The scowl on his face tells me he doesn't appreciate my humor. "Let's get some rest," I yawn. "Looks like we'll need it." Even though my mind is whirling, trying to cope with this new experience my body is giving way to sleep. Gradually it overtakes me. The acrid odor of the floor and the pulsing thoughts vanish from my senses and I sleep. I am oblivious to the cold. My tired body will have its way. I am no longer its master.

Strange voices just outside the barn wake me. They are American voices! They are speaking English! Before I can fully relish the thought of being freed, I realize the shouting of German guards is the more dominant sound and when the barn door is unlocked, we are ushered out to join another group of American prisoners.

There are now over fifty of us and the guards number has increased to six. They offer us no food. A cold dipper of water from an ice encrusted pail will have to suffice for dinner. Roger is angry but there is nothing to be done. We are marched out of the barnyard and down the slippery snow covered road. It is so cold even the movement of walking doesn't seem to trigger any heat within us. We need nourishment to generate heat.

The day grows longer. More prisoners are added to our group. We are not allowed to talk but words are muttered back and forth among the men, comments mostly describing their feelings towards the Germans. By the end of the day, we number close to two hundred prisoners.

"Wonder why there are only able bodied men in this group?" I ask Roger. "No wounded."

"Don't know, Bob, but they must have separated the prisoners for a reason. It's a fact they couldn't march like we are."

"No, and we will start to lose some of these men if we don't get some food pretty soon."

"That's for sure," Roger answers emphatically, "and I'm one of them."

It is beginning to get dark. We are following a country road that meanders from farm to farm. Ahead we can see a German troop truck parked in front of a walled in courtyard. German soldiers are standing in the road, blocking our way. They detour us into the farmer's courtyard and tell us we will spend the night here. That, we find out soon enough, means we sleep out in the open on snow covered ground. We have no blankets. An hour passes and we are roused, shivering and physically exhausted. The German soldiers line us up by the wall and we are given a drink of water from a tin can. As we pass the well, we are each handed a used G I blanket from the German truck. And, as if surprises never cease, we receive a slice of hard black bread. It is our first food in two days and though it isn't much, it relieves our hunger pangs.

Now the huddled group is seated on the ground with blankets wrapped around our heads and shoulders, trailing down the back and held tightly around our knees by chilled hands. We feel warmer and yet we wonder why this sudden change in treatment by our captors. The night passes cold and quiet.

The eerie white darkness of a snow covered courtyard gives way to the chill of dawn's light. Voices of our guards yelling, "Raus! Raus!" interrupts our fitful sleep. The arrogance in their tone shows contempt. I struggle to my feet and slowly move my arms and legs striving to unlock the frigid muscles. They resist all efforts and only through pain and brisk rubbing by stiff fingers can I get them to function.

We are again lined up by the well and as we receive

our drink of water, a count is taken by a German officer. With legs still numb from the cold, we awkwardly walk out to the road. Our day has begun. It is the day before Christmas.

There is no conversation in the ranks as all effort is channeled to keep our feet on the slippery, rutted road. A prisoner's fall is punctuated by a curse as his body is bruised by sharp clods of frozen earth. We march on with a larger complement of guards. Ten in all. They surround us. Their bleak faces showing indifference. They are doing their ordered duty. They have no reason to show emotion.

Our road has finally intersected a highway and a town looms in the distance. As we approach it we see its designated name on a sign proudly proclaiming its existence as Gerolstein. On the outskirts, under a towering rock cliff that overhangs a huge warehouse, we are herded into a fenced area. There we are searched for weapons again and ordered to enter the single door that is dwarfed by the warehouse's high walls. Other prisoner's are already confined in its vastness. They note our entry with anxious questions, hoping to glean some information on the state of the war. We can only tell them of our experiences of the past few days, which compares with their own. They had arrived just hours before us. The best spots along the walls and on the shelved platforms are already occupied. Roger and I sit tiredly on the cement floor.

"Looks like an assembly area for prisoners." I suggest to Roger.

"Yeah, and will you notice all the shoulder patches of the First Army Divisions. I'll bet the 28th doesn't even exist anymore."

As the hours pass, the warehouse receives more and more prisoners until it is completely filled past comfortable capacity. There are over five hundred prisoners here now. Some are wounded. Just at dusk, orders are given to clear out the warehouse. We stand in the fenced enclosure waiting for another march to begin. But instead, near the warehouse door, a line is formed, passing in front of outdoor latrines which we strain to use as it may be our only chance for the night. There is no toilet paper and soon the latrines are a complete mess. Those at the end of the line, after using the facility, are ordered to clean up the entire area.

"Remember, Roger, center of the line. Not the front and not the back from here on in. Let's not get caught on any details! O.K.?" I comment.

"Jawohl," he grunts.

The line continues moving and as it is directed back into the warehouse, we are given a drink of water and a slice of bread. The slice of German bread I now hold in my hand is ice cold and although I am hungry, it does not fill my need for food.

Christmas Eve seems so far away buried in dreams and memories. Memories of past Christmas Eves flood my mind. I miss the excitement of decorating the tree that my brothers and I hauled in on our backs from the woods. I remember the meager snacks and the jokes about hidden presents. But on this Christmas Eve only a cold cement floor in this far away warehouse provides us a space to stretch out and reflect on happier times. The air is filled with the hum of voices. Even a laugh bursts from someone who still doesn't realize the seriousness of his situation. Or does it come from a man who has fully taken stock and found out he must make the best of it for his own morale and for all those around him?

"I don't know if it's just because I'm so hungry or does this bread really taste this good?" Roger questions.

"Both," I answer. "Just wish there was more of it."

"Yeah, like a whole loaf."

There is silence as we munch. Minutes pass. The entire warehouse is almost quiet as we savor each bite, knowing this is all we will have to eat for another twenty-four hours. From a far corner a voice is raised, singing distincty like a bell ringing on a cold clear night. The words are easily recognized with the tune. Others join in. Soon we all are singing:

> Round yon Vir-ir-gin
> Mother and child...

The silence that follows begs for more. Will the voice lead us again? Anxiously we wait, holding our breath. We wish to hear the first words so we can join in as soon as possible. We have raised ourselves to a sitting position to be able to sing easier and to look in the direction of the voice.

Singing was always a part of our Christmas Eve. I can picture my mother seated at the piano, hands poised as we wait for the chord. It gave us our notes for harmony. Now, as my mind focuses on home, the leader in a far corner of the warehouse begins:

Oh little town of Bethlehem
How still we see thee lie...

The emotion of Christmas Eve is upon us. It has brought an awakening to our bodies and a warmth to our hearts. Even in these dark days, those of us who believe, know God is with us.

Jingle bells, jingle bells
Jingle all the way...

Five hundred voices fill the air.

Oh what fun it is to ride
In a one horse open sleigh-eigh...

Hands applaud. Yells of approval are heard. Here and there a shrill whistle of appreciation pierces the air. The evening's glow through the skylight gives us enough illumination to see over the entire group and except for the dark corners, we can see smiles of joy on alot of lightly bearded faces.

I think of Midnight Mass and singing in the choir at the Guardian Angels Church. As I look out over the congregation, I join in their spiritual ardor and I'm inspired to sing for them in the best tenor voice I can muster. Jean is there, sitting with my brothers and friends.

The hidden emotions I now feel are beginning to overwhelm me. How I long for home. I miss all of them so much---.

The guards have entered. They stand near the doorway, rifles slung on their shoulders, a look of anticipation on their faces. They want to hear the Christmas carols also.

Oh come all ye faithful,
Joyful and triumphant...

Suddenly a roar of airplanes above us is followed closely by explosions of the bombs they have dropped. Huge chunks of rock hurdle down through the roof from the overhanging cliff, falling in our midst, crushing those who moments ago were joyfully singing. Men are screaming as more bombs fall, breaking loose another avalanche of rock. Glass from the skylights descend in a shower over us. Dust swirls in dirty clouds as part of the roof caves in. Though no area on the floor is safer than the rest, some men are stumbling over others, rushing to find safety. Roger and I are flat on the floor with our hands over our heads holding onto our helmet liners.

"Geez, what the hell happened? Whose planes are those? Ours? What the hell are they bombing us for?" Roger asks unaware of the sequence of questions he has himself answered.

The roar of the bombers has stopped. Pandemonium, like an epidemic, has spread throughout the warehouse. No one escapes its noisy wrath. Screams and moans are interspersed with curses and voices calling out the names of lost buddies. It is difficult to breath as the clouds of dust settle on us. Both Roger and I have sustained minor cuts from the shards of falling glass that landed on our area. Otherwise we are unhurt.

We listen for more sounds of war other than pitiful cries for help of those near us. Hearing none, I venture to my knees and look about, my eyes blinking in the dusty air. "My God, it's horrible," I exclaim. "Roger! Roger! Let's see if we can help anyone. Come on! Get up! Hurry! Hurry!"

"Where do we start!" All around us prisoners are lifting boards and timbers from men pinned beneath them. Others are using the timbers to pry the huge chunks of rock that hold bodies crushed under them. We rush to help a single man who is gasping for air as he holds a timber up just above his bruised head. He cannot speak. His throat is hurt but we can't see the extent of the damage. Quickly we relieve him of his burden. He waves us on to help others. But there are so many!

Broken legs protrude from the debris. Pools of blood are everywhere and screams for help cannot be answered fast enough. We work as a team, helping as many as we can. Three prisoners are pounding on the door, shouting, "Medic! Medic! Doctor! Doctor! Send us a doctor! Let us out of here!"

Their cries go unanswered. The door remains locked.

The throes of pain are wailed out into the night. The agony of helplessness settles upon us. "What the hell more can we do?" I shout at Roger as we stumble over a man in convulsions. "Here, hold his arms down while I try to grab his tongue. Get his comb out. We can use it as a depresser. Otherwise he may swallow it. Or bite it off. Hurry, Roger, he's biting my fingers. Hurry!"

The prisoner, relaxing as the convulsion passes, opens his eyes and stares into space. His face is blank. His breathing shallow. We leave him and turn to help a man applying a belt as a tourniquet to his badly lacerated right leg. Glass is covering the floor around him and we brush it aside as we tell him to lie down and be still after the tourniquet is tightened. That is all we can do for him.

Moving on, we put our muscles to work lifting rocks, boards and metal roofing. The dead lie beneath the debris.

An hour passes before the door is opened. Guards shout, "Raus! Raus!" pointing to the door. Those of us who can walk are quickly ushered outside to shiver in the fenced area. Eight covered trucks are lined up near the door. Guards are everywhere. Their rifles are at ready and they are in a bad mood. Fright shows on some of their faces but the ones we watch are the ones that walk in a semi-crouch, a maniacal look glowering above their bayoneted rifles. Screams are heard from the warehouse interior. Painful shrieks that cry out unanswered.

The injured are being carried to the trucks. No time has been taken to splint their broken limbs or bandage their open wounds. The pitiful sight is more than some can bear. They turn their heads and vomit. Others are crying openly. We can feel the pain of our comrades but there is nothing we can do. Yet we cannot turn our faces from the atrocity before us.

"Damn," Roger mutters in despair. "How can this happen? On Christmas Eve! Bombed by our own planes!"

"The warehouse isn't marked P.O.W." I pause. "There are German troop trucks in the area and there are a million of our footprints in the snow on the road and inside the fence."

"Yeah, but on Christmas Eve?"

"This afternoon is the first time the clouds and fog

have disappeared enough for our fly boys to see since the attack began. This must look like a troop marshaling area from the sky."

As we talk our eyes are glued to the scene at the door as the trucks pull away. The wailing of voices fades into the night. Two huge flatbed trucks appear from the wooded area behind the warehouse. As they approach the door, we are assembled and stand dumbfounded as the interpreter orders us to enter the warehouse and carry out the dead.

There is resistance at the door and the guards use clubs to stop it. Meekly those men now enter the scene of carnage. The bodies are gently picked up and placed on the truck. We are not allowed to remove their dog tags for identification. There are no further words spoken. The mangled torsos and separated limbs are gathered on sheets of metal roofing and carried through the door. We search under the debris until we are assured that all of the dead are removed. It is over. We cannot look each other in the eye. Heads are bowed. Tears flow freely. The living mourn the dead. We are exhausted.

Roger rests on a fallen timber. I must remain standing a little longer for in my mind, if I sit, it will be a sign of resignation to what we have just witnessed. I cannot release the enormity of it. Roger's hand touches mine as he says, "Sit down, Bob. There is nothing we can do."

The futility of our situation is magnified as the guards enter the wretched building. "You must clear all this out, now!" the interpreter shouts pointing to the glass, rocks, metal sheets and boards.

"Raus! Raus!"

Dejectedly we move the piles of debris. Load after load is carried out to a corner of the fenced enclosure. Large rocks are rolled onto metal roofing sheets and dragged away. Some rocks are so huge we cannot budge them. Only these, bloody stains and dust are left on the floor. It is Christmas Day.

The sun is beaming through the jagged holes in the roof. Outside the snow is melting, washing away our footprints and the blood stains of last night. Roger and I sleep wrapped tightly in our blankets.

66

While we are sleeping, more prisoners are brought into the warehouse. Our tired bodies do not acknowledge the noise they make. We sleep deeply, exhausted both physically and mentally from last night's ordeal.

The bright sun directly overhead shines warmly on my face through the holes in the roof. Its light on my eyes slowly awaken me and as I look about, I am amazed to see so many men. The floor is crowded. There isn't enough room for everyone to lie down. As I sit up, a tired looking boy of maybe eighteen years, sits where my legs were stretched out. He smiles in appreciation.

"Where did all of you come from?" I question.

"We've been on the road for four days and nights," he wheezes, which leads to a hacking cough.

I don't want to make him talk any more for fear he will cough in my face. Roger is awake now and stretches as he groans. "Looks like we got company. Hope they brought breakfast."

Christmas afternoon passes quickly. Our minds are occupied with securing enough room to lie down again. At dusk we are ordered outside. We use the latrine, share the common tin can for a drink of water and receive a slice of heavy black bread. All the planning of space has been lost as Roger and I head for the center of the floor and sit facing each other, our legs extended. Soon the warehouse is filled. The only ones left outside are the surprised new prisoners who have been chosen for the latrine clean up detail. The men around us are talking and eating their bread. Not a crumb is wasted.

A pudgy man next to me produces a deck of cards and soon six of us are deeply involved in a potless poker game which continues until we can no longer see. Nothing to do but sleep. It easily overtakes us.

Days pass in repetition. We use glass chips for our bets while playing poker. It occupies our endless hours. The bombers come over regularly, sometimes dropping explosives and sometimes they pass us by. We no longer pay any attention to them. The Germans have not marked the building with the letters P.O.W and therefore it still looks like any other partially damaged German warehouse with a lot of activity surrounding it. We realize our planes are duty bound to destroy these sites.

There are now over six hundred prisoners jammed together in the building. Some can find no place to sit and though they are dead on their feet, no one offers them their place to sit. Sick men, wounded men, tired men and dirty men afraid to die yet they are more afraid of what life as a prisoner of war holds in store for them.

After each bombing the German SS squads come and take away a group of prisoners. The rumor is that they dispose of them in retaliation for the destruction our Air Force has dealt their country. Already we have heard of their gas chambers where prisoners, Jews, political dissidents and intellectuals are done away with. Promised showers, they are herded into a room where gas comes out of hidden vents. Another vicious German torture has taken its toll. Their bodies are then stacked like cord wood out in the open, buried or cremated to mask the heinous deed. I think, "Do they revel in attempting to build a super race? Can they justify in their hearts these wanton massacres? Why do they both flaunt it and hide it? Do they have to prove to the German people that the military is not wasting precious food from the country's meager supplies?"

The other poker players with Roger and I discuss the aspect of the situation. We cannot decide on an answer to it because it does not follow a pattern. It seems as though it all depends upon the individual in command of the immediate area. But then, someone must be issuing the directives! Our minds are called back to the card game as the dealer spreads out a royal flush.

At the end of a week in the warehouse, even the card game is boring. The stench of unclean bodies and the aching of stiff muscles are beginning to make men irritable. It is near the time for our nightly sojourn and so Roger and I stand and stretch before picking our way over tangled arms and legs, gaining a spot close to the door. The sooner we are outside the more time we will have to walk and to breath fresh air.

The door opens and a detail of guards enter, their rifles at ready. A tall authoritative guard calls for silence. "Ach-tung!"

When the babble of voices in the far corners has stopped and all prisoners are standing, their shuffling feet noiseless, he asks in perfect English, "How many of you feel you could walk ten miles to a real Stalag: a prison camp where you will be housed in barracks and receive three meals a day, have church services every Sunday and a permanent address where you could write and receive mail from home?" He and his attending guards rush from the building as six hundred men stampede toward them to be first on the list. Those of us in front are crushed against the wall. The door is closed and locked. I cannot breath. My arm is pressed against a sharp projection from the wall and the pain is excruciating. Slowly, agonizingly, the pressure is released as the men back off.

"Christ," Roger pants, "we'll be killed by our own men!"

We wait by the wall. There is still the hope of fresh air and bread. The door is again flung open. An SS officer, pistol in hand, surrounded by more guards, stands framed by sun light. He motions us forward. The first forty men are to be the selected few.

Chapter Four

As I look at Roger, I pray we have made the right decision. The thirty-eight other men are energetically swinging their arms and flexing their knees preparing for the ten mile hike.

"ACH-TUNG," the officer bellows. We stand before him as his eyes intently take inventory of our physical condition. Satisfied with what he sees, we are directed over to the latrine. Next comes the tin can drink of water followed by our nightly ration of bread.

"Ten miles to go." The thought floods my brain as we stride out of the fenced area with six Germans guarding us. Twenty-four hours later there cannot be a more disillusioned group this side of the Rhine. We have marched continuously for over thirty miles with nothing to eat or drink. Only one stop to change guards.

Late in the evening we approach a city that has columns of smoke pouring upward. Plumes of crimson flare in the eastern sky. Crimson is reflected on the great bank of cumulus clouds that hang along the hills. Shadows lay gaunt and ominous before the buildings untouched by the holocaust of fire and destruction. Though our bombers have dropped their load hours ago, the wind whips sparks and soot in a frenzy which seems to signify its loathe in stopping its role in this destruction. I shudder involuntarily as the guards accelerate our pace. This is our first confrontation with people whose homes and families have just been destroyed. People who are suffering horribly.

Cobbled streets ring a tattoo under our shoes. The men are noticeably forming closer ranks as if gaining strength to view the scene. There is a sick feeling in the pit of our stomachs. A German officer if striding toward us, his face as red as the flames that lick the side of the old frame buildings. Purple veins stand out on his nose as he speaks with authority to the guards.

Pointing to the North, his gestures giving an air of utter contempt for us, his orders are loud and fast. We immediately detour up a side street in the direction he has pointed. Leading the way with his swagger stick slapping his shiny boot tops, the officer looks neither right nor left at the homes gutted by fire. His mind is a blank to human feeling and only one idea fills the brain beneath the pointed cap. We follow him to the railroad yards where the sight is one huge rat race of German civilians trying to salvage what they can from the burning box cars. Bomb craters are everywhere. Twisted rails with their ends curling toward the sky make the scene seem unreal. It looks like a modern painting that makes sense only to the artist.

As Roger and I pick our way through the destruction, I wonder how and if this railroad can ever be used again. "Will they ever get all of these bomb craters filled so they can even start to repair the damage?"

We are assigned ten men to a hole and told to start working. The shovels they hand us are worn out from their constant work of filling bomb craters. They are old hands at it. Only the men now wielding them are new to the performance. One prisoner, who speaks a little "school book German," protests to the German officer that prisoners of war are not required to do this labor for them because it is connected with military operations.

The swagger stick cuts across his face, rubberizing his knees and he slumps to the ground. Again and again the German officer raises the stick and slashes the prisoner's head. The guards have pushed the safeties off their rifles and stand ready for a riot. When the officer finishes venting his anger on him, the prisoner's head is a mass of bloody welts.

We now realize we are not only prisoners of war but also prisoners of our captor's abuse. Curses are muttered from the angry crowd of civilians surrounding us and we are lost in our thoughts as to what course we should take. Before we can regain our composure the guards push four men to work digging. We follow their move. Six hours and twelve bomb craters later brings us our first break. We are still on our feet by sheer mind over matter. I think, "It is amazing how much the human body can endure."

We have moved twisted rails and splintered ties, thrown tons of broken cement in the holes and as soon as one is filled, we move to another. The past twenty-four hours have been a nightmare to our bodies. I look at Roger, a well proportioned man with an ever ready smile. His light brown hair and beady eyes gleam in the night as if

71

they are fired with electricity. His smile flashes and he pants, "We're not going to let them get us down over a little thing like this, are we?"

Too exhausted to speak, I shake my head for an answer.

The guards summon us away from the civilian work area just as we see a hand-pulled cart turn the corner and proceed to the center of the railroad yard. Hot, steaming kettles of food are uncovered and served to the men and women. We are ordered to sit in the snow next to the fence-line that surrounds the area.

Our guards take turns going to the cart and having their mess kits filled. They stand in a semi-circle around us eating and laughing. At the order, "Raus!" we rise and are marched toward the cart. The civilians stand aside, eyeing us contemptuously, yet tolerating our need for nourishment. A tin can of soup and a slice of bread is handed to each of us. The German officer, overseeing the portions, coldly eyes us as we pass before him.

Later, with the sun rising on our left, we are again slogging our way down a country road, mud splashing at each step. The tin cans that held our soup are now empty but we clutch them possessively. Our road had been torn up from excessive use by large vehicles; supplies and troops being rushed to the front. Back country roads are safer these days with our Air Force bombing depots and searching for convoys.

By mid-morning Roger and I are reciting a list of towns and villages we have marched through. It may be our only sense of escape if the opportunity should arise. "Gerolstein, Schutz, Deudesfeld, Bettenfeld, Gelsdorf and Herforst."

Across the open fields I can see roof tops of barns and houses. As we draw closer, one building stands out. It is square and two stories high with a few windows. Not a large building but it draws my eye because it is so different from the rest. Red bricks form the walls with a large smoking chimney the only break in its relief. Farm houses surround it with fields and forests beyond on the horizon. A small wooden sign in need of paint proclaims the village name, "Heidweiler."

We are halted in front of the red brick building, which we can clearly see is a former schoolhouse. The front door is set near the right side of the wall. It opens and a group of German soldiers exit, lining up on each side of the short sidewalk. We are led through the open door and up a stairway that hugs the wall. The door at the head of the stairs opens to a rectangular room that encompasses the width of the back of the school. "Have we reached our destination?"

The door is closed behind us and we are left alone in the room that contains only a pot-bellied stove. The one window in the back wall, next to the chimney, is boarded up. The wooden floor is approximately twenty-four feet long and eighteen feet wide. It is too late for Roger and me to gain wall space as the men rush to claim areas. We are almost in the center of the room and join the others on the floor stretching out to establish our boundaries.

We roll out our folded blanket and place our helmet liner and tin can on it. The mumble of voices in the room is stifled as the door opens and a hulking brute of a man enters. His uniform does not fit him properly and his huge right hand holds his rifle as if it were a small stick. His face is ugly with pig-like eyes and a flattened nose. His mere presence commands quiet. Two more soldiers appear at his side, their rifles held at ready.

"Schmidt!" he calls out, looking over the prisoners. From the back corner, near the stove, a prisoner rises to his feet. The two men stare at each other for a moment. The guard, speaking German with his gutteral accent, gives a rambling diatribe.

Schmidt interprets for us. "He says he is the head of our new guards. I don't know what his rank is. This is to be our stalag for now. We can rest for what's left of the day but tomorrow we will work. I don't know how he got my name or how they knew I speak German, but I am to be your dolmetscher, or interpreter." Schmidt turns to the German and waits for further orders. There are none. The three guards exit.

"What the hell is this?" a voice from across the room shouts. "This is no barracks. And I'll bet we don't get three meals a day either!"

Schmidt answers, "I don't know anymore than you do. Looks to me like we've been suckered into a labor gang."

"What are we going to do about it?"

"Don't look like we've got much of a choice, does it?" Schmidt's voice shows signs of resignation.

Roger coughs and hold his throat. "Sure feels sore," he complains. He covers himself with his blanket and using his field jacket for a pillow, quickly falls asleep. In a moment I am also covered and asleep The room is warm and dry, a comfort after the past weeks.

"Schmidt, schnell!" the loud voice brings us back to life as we stir under our blanket. The ugly guard shouts again. "Schmidt, schnell! Kommen -- brot." Schmidt quickly steps over men still laying down as he threads his way to the door. The guard hands him six loaves of bread and, speaking in German, tells him to distribute it to the men.

"Six loaves," Schmidt says. "Six loaves. How can we divide six loaves between forty men?"

"Easy," I answer. "Give four loaves to four groups of ten men each. That leaves two loaves. Cut them in half and give each group a half. If the loaf is cut into ten slices and the half is cut into five slices and then cut again in half, each man will have one and a half slices." Some of the men have figured it out while others sit dumbfounded. The room is divided into four sections.

"Anyone got a knife?" Schmidt asks. Laughter breaks out. There are no knives in this group after all the searches we've been through. Two men produce pieces of metal strapping about eight inches long.

"Found these at the rail yard," one flatly states. "Don't know if they're sharp enough to cut bread and they're rusty but they'll have to do."

Schmidt rubs the metal pieces against the stove and soon most of the rust has disappeared. After wiping the blades against his pants leg, he begins to slice the two loaves in half. Each group then uses the metal "knives" to divide the bread as equally as possible.

Roger swallows in pain as the coarse bread scratches his throat. "Damn," he says, "didn't ever think I'd have trouble eating."

A question is asked as a man raises his voice, "What kind of work are we going to be doing tomorrow?"

"We're professionals at filling bomb holes in railway yards," laughs a happy voice next to Roger. "Course, I don't think this village has too many trains." A few of

74

the men chuckle at the man's remarks.

"What's your name?" Schmidt asks.

Before the man can answer, a voice from the stove area shouts, "Joker." Now all are laughing and the man will from now on be known as "Joker."

"Maybe they will turn us all into farmers?" drawls a tall lanky man.

"That's fine with me," Roger states. "One way or other I'll find enough to eat on a farm." His grin turns into a painful look as he coughs again. "And my name is Roger."

Discussion groups form as the work we are to begin tomorrow becomes the topic of conversation. The early evening hours pass quickly and suddenly the one bare ceiling light is turned off by the guards. It is time for sleep. Snores and gurgles fill the air. We are tired.

All too soon the light is turned on and the door opens.

"Raus! Raus!" the guard shouts.

We are rushed out of the room and down the stairs. Lining up in front of the school in two ranks, cold and still half asleep, we realize it is just past dawn. I can hear a rooster crowing in the distance and dogs barking.

One rank at a time is led behind the schoolhouse where an outside spigot provides us with a drink of ice cold water. Standing in the doorway by the spigot is the German cook, a large man in a dirty white apron. He watches us carefully as he sips a cup of steaming coffee. Soon we are all lined up in front of the school and are told to follow the guards.

Walking down the rutted road that leads through Heidweiler, we pass barns and houses that are one story high, built of logs, board siding and stucco. Our left rank, led by guards, is detoured into a farm yard that contains a large long wooden building. Roger and I are in the right rank and continue through the village. At the outskirts we can see two huge wagons pulled by oxen. They are on our road and we follow them into the fields for a mile before reaching a forest. The oxen are driven into the woods where they reach a turnaround. Roger points to a pile of logs on the hillside and says, "I'll bet that's our work."

Soon the ox-drawn wagons return, coming to a stop facing us. They are larger than any oxen I've ever seen.

They stand as tall as my head and their necks are heavy and powerful from their life of hard work. Billows of steam snort from their nostrils as they patiently wait for us to load their wagons and for the whip to descend, starting them off to the village.

We are led up the hill and told to pick up a log and carry it to the wagon. The hardwood logs are about eight feet long and from six to ten inches in diameter. Roger and I struggle to balance one on our shoulders and soon find out from the guards that we are EACH expected to carry a log! Though we do not believe we can do this, we soon are part of a line slowly placing our feet one at a time on the treacherous hillside, keeping our footing and balancing the log with two hands that will throw the log off our shoulder should we slip.

The first trip is exhausting. Four men are kept at the wagons to load the logs while the rest of us are started up the hill again for another load. We can see two more ox wagons coming from the village. They will arrive about the same time as our two are loaded.

The wood has been previously cut and stacked. Only selected trees are harvested. I can see the arranged plantings of their ever military country. When we were crossing the field, I could not see into the woods. The trees were as thick as hair on a dog's back but now when I look toward the open area from the woods, I can see the fields of fire carefully planned.

All morning we are kept moving. Up and down the hill we plod, carrying snow encrusted frozen logs. Our strength is fading, leaving us with sheer will power to do the work. At mid-day we are halted and told to sit. The last wagon to arrive brought food for the guards and the aroma of this food makes us even hungrier.

We name the guards as we sit in a semi-circle watching them eat. The fat, bald headed one is called, "Skinhead." Next to him sits, "The Brute," his pig eyes and powerful physique presenting us with a reminder to stay clear. "Popeye" is an older man with a long thin face, one blind eye and a pipe in his mouth. He and "Chipmunk" seem to hit it off good together. The latter has two buck teeth that could eat an apple through a snow fence. By him sits "Eightball. He doesn't comprehend too well and because

76

of that he is always the point of jokes from the guards. The other two are not German. The prisoner sitting in front of me says he heard they are Polish and have been forced into the German Army. One has a large scar on his jaw, probably from a bayonet, that seems to affect his speech. The other walks with a limp because he was shot in the leg. These seven guard us in the woods. We note other German soldiers on sentry duty, posted near the approaches to the village.

The hot soup brought out to the guards is noisily being slurped by them. The breeze wafts the soup kettle's aroma directly to us and groans are heard from those who cannot control their hunger. Roger and I look at each other and shake our heads. It is better to forget the soup we will not be eating. As the guards finish their bread and soup, they reach for cigarettes which we notice are "Lucky Strikes."

"Well, so much for Red Cross Parcels," I whisper dejectedly. "You know where they have been going."

"Yeah," Roger answers, "I wonder who is supposed to check on these things? Some international board or something."

"Well, almost the whole world is at war so the countries can't spare the help for minor details," I state in exasperation.

The guards finish their smoke and leeringly look at us as they stomp and twist their boots on the butts, as if to say, "Don't even think of us leaving one for you."

The glowing sun fades on the horizon before we are told to follow the last load of logs to the village. The relief gives us enough strength to slowly plod behind the creaking wagons. When we are partially through town, the wagons are turned into the farmyard where the other prisoners are working. We must unload the logs before joining the other prisoners on the march back to the schoolhouse.

Up the stairs we stumble, staggering through the doorway and falling on the floor where our blankets lie. Exhaustion overtakes us. The great fatigue does not allow for conversation. Roger coughs uncomfortably and clutches at his throat. I can tell he is in great pain but there is nothing I can do to help him except wrap a blanket around his shoulders.

Bread is brought in and carefully sliced to make each portion equal. I join the line to get a can of drinking water from the faucet at the back of the building. God, how my muscles ache. My hands are torn and raw. Washing them off with a handful of snow on the way back from the barnyard brings numb relief but now they burn with pain. As I stand in line, shoes and socks soaked through to my cold feet, I wonder, "How long can we keep up this forced labor? And Roger? He is suffering a painful sore throat."

Returning to our room with a can of cold water, I join Roger and we slowly munch on our bread. Little conversation is heard as there is no energy left in our weary bodies. Some men are already sleeping. They do not wait for the light to go out signaling sack time. Roger coughs painfully, groping for his throat as if his hands can soothe the swollen area. He is helpless in his suffering.

I cover him with the blanket and we're soon asleep, our aches and pains overwhelmed by our exhaustion.

"Raus! Raus!" startles us as we open our eyes and blink from the glare of the light bulb above us. Morning already! Roger does not attempt to sit up. His throat is so swollen; he can hardly breath.

"Schmidt," I call out, "come here." As he approaches, I tell him, "Look at Roger's throat. He can't work today. Tell the guards he must stay inside and they must give him some medication."

"I'll tell them but I don't know if they care or not."

The door opens. "Schnell!" Popeye shouts, his eye circling the room. Schmidt calls to Popeye as I walk to the door and follow the men down the stairs and out into the freezing grey morning air. With the morning ritual finished, we are again marched out to the woods to complete another day of hauling logs. Roger does not join us. I thank God for His mercy.

Bruised and tired we plod behind the oxen, back to the farmyard. There we unload the two wagons at the end of our day. Walking to the schoolhouse my pains are forgotten, as I think of Roger and his condition. My cold wet shoes remind me that I should have removed Roger's before I left this morning so they could dry out.

Chapter Five

In the morning Roger will be gone! God only knows where.

"The guards say they are taking you to a hospital?"

He nods his head.

"Hospital, hah! It's about time they got you out of this stinking room," I mumble. "They shouldn't have us working as hard as we are with so little food, soaking wet shoes, no gloves or mittens... Soon we will all be in the same condition, ready for the hospital."

An almost inaudible raspy curse follows another cough. Roger is badly in need of a doctor. If only I could believe they will take him to receive help.

He has not been able to eat all of his bread ration for two days. Its coarseness scratches his swollen throat to the point where it has started to bleed and so he put it under his helmet liner that is now his pillow. I think he has strep throat, pneumonia and a few other complications all jammed between his tongue and chest. Even if my eyes could pierce through his beard, his features would be indistinguishable. The glands in his neck are swollen and hot to the touch. They are puffed out so much that I'm sure if he pricked the area with a pin, it would explode.

If only I can get him to eat a few bites, he may have a chance to make the trip tomorrow and still stay alive. They have made us walk hundreds of miles around their bomb blasted country and they may make him walk tomorrow.

I pull my blanket high about my shoulders as I hunch forward trying to make the blanket cover my chilled legs. My thoughts continue. "What should I do? Am I more concerned over whether Roger is going to be shot, placed in a gas chamber, used as a guinea pig in their notorious experiments, or is it that I cannot believe I am to be left alone in this slave labor group of P.O.W.'s?" They are about their own business, sleeping, scratching, or as I am, glassy eyed in a dream of their own. Characters? All of them!

I've not taken the time to get to know them. I talk with them, work with them, suffer with them, starve with them but I really know very little about them. Roger and I are close friends, sharing our thoughts and looking out for each other. It's going to be so different now. Looking over at him, I can't help but shake my head and wonder if he will be taken care of.

"Would war be changed, Rog, if the planners suddenly had to go in the game as a substitute for the players? Now there's one for the experts. Let them try to come up with an answer to that!"

Roger shakes his head negatively. This action brings on another persistent siege of coughing and spitting which interrupts my thoughts. I drop the blanket from my shoulders and reach out to hold his head a little higher to ease the pain that racks his throat and chest. He is a poorly dressed specimen of a soldier. Shoes with the soles torn half off, pants ripped and filthy from work he can no longer do, sweat stained underwear that is coming apart at its rotting seams. He holds his throat with his left hand while scratching his waist with his right.

"Hey, Rog, those lice getting to you again? Guess I had better delouse your clothes tonight. If I don't, they will multiply so fast you'll never get ahead of them on your own when you leave tomorrow." I scratch under my own belt to relieve the sudden itching.

"When he leaves..." That thought enters my mind again. There, facing me, is the terrible fact: I'm a prisoner of war. And soon I won't have a friend like Roger to lean on. It will be a further strain on my already tense nerves. Taking a deep breath to control my feelings, I find I must blink my eyes to hold back the tears. I have to do something to comfort both of us.

Automatically I gaze upward. "Oh God, what can I do to comfort these men? I'm only nineteen. We're prisoners. We're starving little by little. We're tired. Our spirits are broken. Some of us no longer care if we live another day..."

There is no answer.

Whenever I feel the knife of despair cutting through my confidence and my thoughts begin to surrender to a degrading hopelessness, I look at the ring Jean gave me. It's her class ring, given with all her love. Now as I caress the golden circle, I cherish it with loving tenderness, recalling a world I hardly remember.

A thought comes to me. It is an idea that should be far from my mind and yet it storms my conscience and my conscience gives its permission. I must try to trade the ring for food so that Roger can gain enough strength to endure the trip tomorrow. If I can get the guard to let me go for a can of drinking water, maybe the cook will be greedy enough to make a trade. I lower Roger's head and quickly go to the door.

After a few words and hand signals, I manage to make the guard understand I want a drink of water. He shouts to the outside guard who is at the foot of the stairs that I am coming out. The cold night air, unbearably cold even for mid-January, penetrates my threadbare clothes and I shiver as I walk alongside the building. I hesitate before I step around the corner of the converted school. "Do I really have enough courage to trade Jean's ring for food? Will she ever realize that at this moment I have to make a decision that will affect my conscience for the rest of my life?"

I walk into the dimly lit room. The cook glances up and jumps to his feet, his hairy chest glistening through the sweat in his unbuttoned underwear. Before he can shout for the guards, I hold up the ring and point to his poorly stocked shelves of food. His eyes glare at the ring as I make him understand I wish to trade it for food.

He takes the ring and asks, "Frau?"

"Yes," I answer.

I would rather have his hands at my throat than touching Jean's ring. His hoarse voice, muttering guttural words, brings back my attention as he hands me one slice of bread. Throwing the bread on the table, I use hand signals and some German words to explain that Roger is sick and cannot swallow the coarse bread. "I want some hot soup or broth!"

He looks at me with a fierceness that brings back my courage again. I stare at him, not backing off. It's a wonder he doesn't call the guard and have me shot, making an example of me to the other prisoners. I am aware of the beads of sweat on my forehead and a weakening in my knees. I am frightened more than when their 88's were pounding our foxholes. The cook, taking a small flour sack, stuffs two loaves of bread and some crusts into it. Then, pushing it into my hands, shoves me outside and closes the door behind me. I wonder how hard he would have shoved me if he had seen the chunk of butter I slid under my shirt while he was filling the sack?

It is quite dark now and the guard outside cannot see the small sack as I pass. "What about the guard at the head of the stairs?" Again I feel this is the end! He will surely think I stole it from the kitchen. The cook won't back me up and admit he has traded it for a ring!

Entering the hallway, I look up. No guard. He is gone! Probably into the guards' room which is opposite ours at the head of the stairs. Quietly I run up the steps, enter our room and shut the door. Beads of sweat stand out on my forehead as I attempt to regulate my heavy breathing. Most of the men are secure in an exhausted sleep. A few glance up and eye the sack in my arms. I reach Roger just in time to watch another attack of coughing tear at his chest and throat. I set the sack of bread down and cover Roger with his jacket.

Thank God they let us bring a few small branches back to our room each day to feed the fire. Picking up the small tin can we use for drinking, I step to the stove and turn around, facing the bread sack. It's still there. With this group of hungry men it's like a lighted billboard that flashes. "HERE IS ONE MONTH'S RATION OF FOOD - THAT FOOL LEFT IT SETTING IN THE MIDDLE OF THE FLOOR." Weakly acknowledging human nature, I have to assume they will never suspect it to be food so carelessly handled.

I bend to my immediate problem. I keep one eye on the bread sack while scraping at the greasy butter on the inside of my shirt. I remove all that is possible. The butter melts quickly in the can on the stove. I return to the bread sack. Taking the freshest loaf, it is dated as being baked one year ago, I break it in half, dig out the center and crumble it into the hot butter.

With Roger's head on my lap, I carefully place the gruel between his parched lips with my fingers and wait while it is slowly swallowed. As I feed him, his eyes fill with tears of pain and yet they thank me. He knows he has to have food for strength, otherwise all the work of planning the trip to the hospital will be a waste of time.

After feeding Roger, he sleeps. I collect my thoughts

as I lay on the cold floor.

Maybe my body in its run down condition is finally beginning to give into the elements. I have made up my mind weeks ago that my good physical condition will carry me through. I weighed one hundred and seventy-five pounds then and felt as though I could lick the whole Kraut population. The Army had really built me up with calisthenics and a proper training program. But now I can feel this prisoner's life tearing all that down.

Slowly I raise myself off the cold hardwood floor and step to the boarded window. In a second I have jerked out the nails we have loosened on the bottom board and noiselessly remove it from the casing. The morning pre-dawn is grey and bleak with wintry blasts howling around the corners of the prison. A noise at the side of the building catches my attention. Peering into the street I can see a horse and wagon convoy of supplies moving slowly through the drifted streets.

"Our Air Force must really be knocking out the German truck supply convoys if they now have to resort to these substitutes." I wonder, "How many of these horses are killed, before reaching their destination and eaten?" As I continue to examine the street, I cannot see what I hope will be there. My view is obstructed by a few buildings.

"Please Lord, make them have the decency to provide a truck or some type of sheltered transportation for Roger."

Replacing the board over the window, I again step over the huddled forms sleeping in their clothes. Some of them still have their shoes on. Distrusting souls. Surely they don't think anyone would take them! That's a laugh. There are some men here that will steal your heart if they think it can be traded for food or cigarettes. I lie down on our blanket, thinking of what I will do when Roger is gone.

"Why does a man get so attached to another? I suppose that's why the Army never lets two men stay together very long during training or at the front. It will surely affect their performance if something happens to one of them. Well, they don't have that to worry about in our division. If a man was on the spear point of the First Army for more than three weeks without being shot up, he was lucky. I am one of those lucky ones."

83

"Maybe they will change all that in the next war. What a thought. The next war! Here I am in a German labor camp trying to keep my body and soul together and I am thinking of the next war. Well, as long as there are greedy, atheistic maniacs on earth, there will be war."

"War is caused by sin." I wonder further, "Where did the word 'war' come from? Probably some Latin derivative from a word meaning to 'covet their neighbor's goods.' I'll have to look that up if I ever get out of this hellhole."

The door bursts open and the words, "Raus! Raus!" jerk the men from oblivion. Another day in "Ye Olde Wood Lot" as we call it.

Our daily meal, consisting of bread, was passed out last night, so this morning as usual, everyone will stand in line to get his drink of water for breakfast.

I wait until the last moment to say good-bye to Roger. Words will not come. We just sit and look at the floor. If only they had taken him first. Now it is as if I am the one that is leaving instead of him. It shouldn't make any difference but it does. He won't take the bread that is left. Says if he is really going to a hospital he won't need it and if... well, he wouldn't need it anyway.

He looks worse than ever this morning and I wonder if I will ever see him again.

Once, in the foxholes, I had a mysterious feeling come over me. When I looked at the man next to me, his face looked wax-like. Fifteen minutes later his life was snuffed out by a German rifleman. During the following weeks it happened the same way, a dozen or more times. Every time I saw them shortly before, that waxy expression was on their face. "Could I honestly have told them they were going to die? What am I thinking! If I had said that, they would have shipped me back to the nurses with a section eight."

Shaking my head to clear my thoughts, reality brings me back to the prison. I look at Roger as I rise to leave. He doesn't have that wax-like look on his face and somehow I feel better. I try to match his smile and we both laugh. He tells me to keep my chin up and we will see each other soon. I stumble down the steps. Tears freeze on my beard as I march down the road with the work detail.

Today I am in the left rank and we are detoured into the farmer's yard that has a huge warehouse. We are given the job of sawing the logs into small wheels, two inches thick. The wheels are chopped into blocks about the size toys stores sell as playthings for children. Already our labor gang has filled the warehouse with these chips of wood. After being converted into charcoal, the Germans burn them in their trucks to provide power. A large tank, set on the side of the truck, is loaded with this fuel and burned to provide steam. We can easily ascertain that Germany has an acute gas shortage.

There is only one buzz saw. Powered by a mixture of low grade kerosene, it roars into action at the beginning of the day and will cough and misfire all day long. It takes two men to keep the belt on and keep the motor running while two more try to wear a log through the dull blade. We could sharpen the blade, tighten the belt and time the motor but that would be to their advantage, so we don't mention it. It is a joke to the men running the buzz saw.

Next to them, in the barnyard of the frustrated old German farmer whose property is taken over for this cavalcade of progress, two men can be seen worrying a hardwood log to pieces with a dull crosscut saw. One handle keeps coming off and the other end has no handle at all. A stick pushed through a hole drilled where the handle is supposed to be, serves its purpose. The pride of the farm-yard operation is an eight inch homemade bench saw, driven by a one third horsepower electric motor. It cuts smoothly but we can only cut part way through the log and then turn it and cut again. At no time are we able to cut a full slice off a log, even after turning it. These logs are called "Totem Poles" because they are sawed every two inches and then a man will chip what he can from it. Then the heart of the log has to be run through the saw again to finally reduce it to the finished product.

Next in line come the "Apprentices." Three men, who command two hand saws and an over-sized keyhole saw, work together on one sawbuck. I did not see them reduce one log to blocks during the entire course of the day.

The "freight wagon," used to haul these blocks to the storage place is another ingenious invention. It is built low with two iron wheels in front and runners in the rear. The wheels are supposed to break trail for the runners in the snow. Four men pull this wagon-sled around the barnyard, shoveling it full of chips with a worn pitchfork. When loaded it holds about six bushels. It is finally dumped in the warehouse.

Only once have we seen a huge truck stop and be loaded with our work. The guards load it. I imagine they do not want us near their only smoothly running piece of machinery in the whole village.

At mid-day the guards' noon meal is over and so we return to work.

I wonder if Roger has been taken away? Maybe they are just telling him about a hospital so he will go peaceably. They have used that ruse before. He must be thinking of the many times they have made promises with no thought of carrying them out. At first they promise big things such as that swell prison camp. Since then, just the promise of a bath or an extra crust of bread can get the same results. Most of us try not to listen to them anymore. The temptation is great because for once they may not be lying.

The afternoon is long and cold. Finally the last load of logs is seen turning into the barnyard. Tired prisoners plod behind the oxen that grunt at every bump as the heavy wooden yoke jams tightly against their front shoulders. Mammoth beasts these oxen, but at the end of a day such as this, they too must welcome their humble stable. The whip cracks constantly in the driver's hand, cutting their powerful flanks, but they will go no faster. With their heads down and eyes closed most of the time, they plod on. Even in our tired minds, we feel sorry for them. They are as much a prisoner as we.

The men unload the logs and leave the empty wagons in the barnyard as we slowly march to our prison, the schoolhouse. I had often thought of school as a prison when I was a boy. Now it is a reality.

I hope Roger is still its prisoner.

Chapter Six

Entering the room, I can see a huddled heap in the center of the floor. Quickly I cross the dimly lit area and stop short, kneeling to lift up the blanket that I think covers Roger. He is gone! There is my bread sack! He has covered it with our blanket so no one will take it.

I have to be called to get our loaves of bread from the guards. A numb brain tries to control my movement as I stumble to the door. The bread is like lead in my hand and yet my subconscious mind speaks for my stomach and I hold on to it.

I must have fainted because I am now in a strange part of the room, almost under the window. Faces are peering at me through a haze and a voice is talking softly as my wrists are being rubbed raw by callused hands. Circulation is restored. The chafing stops as I pull my hands free. The voice is much stronger now, asking, "How do you feel?"

Before I can answer, I slip into a deep sleep. During the night as I awake with a feeling of being watched, I find a young man about my age sitting alongside me, a smile on his bearded face. It is a handsome face that conveys a feeling of friendship and understanding. "Would you like a drink of water, Bob?" he asks pressing a tin can to my lips and pouring the cool water slowly while I drink.

The slice of bread is still in my hand and I bite into it with a feeling of insatiable hunger. Looking at the man beside me, I utter with my mouth full of bread, "Thanks for taking care of me."

Very sincerely he responds, "I watched you taking care of Roger for the past week and thought you deserved the same."

My eyes blink with amazement to think that someone with all his own problems has taken the time to think of me.

"I wanted to join you two weeks ago," he pauses, "but now that Roger has left, I thought maybe you and I could work together?"

While he is talking I try to judge his character and though I have no right to, I find I am comparing him to Roger. His smile flashes on and off with ease, drawing attention to his perfectly matched white teeth. His clothes, though wrinkled and dirty, somehow have a look of neatness about them. This stands out in his favor as some of the men have no sense of cleanliness and self respect left in them. His brown hair is as clean as can be expected and is combed, not tangled and stringy like some of the others. A sort of warmth radiates from him and I know I have found a new friend. He is still talking. The words, "...share everything..." bring me back to the present.

I look for my bread sack, wondering if my character reading has been wrong! The bread sack is alongside me. Evidently he secured it and my blanket during the night.

His voice ringing in my ears, states, "If we do join forces, remember, you had the bread before we met and it's yours. I don't want any of it. Don't think I want to join you because of it. That's why I couldn't contact you today. I knew last night Roger was leaving and I wanted to talk to you about us getting together. I couldn't because you had the bread; it would look quite obvious that my purpose was solely that. Then, tonight when you blanked out, I had my eyes on you because I've been trying to think of some excuse to break the ice. As you started to keel over, I was the only one who noticed. After I caught you, I realized the ice was broken and here we are." He extends his hand and I meet it half way. "The name is Jack," he announces, "Jack Thompson."

The wind howls at the corners of the building but I feel a little of the coldness leave the room. Maybe tomorrow won't be as endless as I have imagined. A small group of men in the center of the room spread out to take up the place Roger and I had called, "ours."

The quiet of the night is disturbed by identifiable noises. Due to the heavy frost, nails in the roof "pop." From the grunting below, I know another convoy of wagoned supplies is inching its way toward the front. These efforts seem wasted to my mind. "Even if most of them complete their trip, it will be such a small donation toward what is needed? How do they think they can supply a modern army this way? Do the Germans dream of the 'good old days' when they drove powerful trucks and rode trains hauling tons of material? Where each snowdrift across the road meant a challenge to the might of their convoy, instead of the blockades they now form for the wagons."

I wonder, "Do they have relay teams of horses up ahead to replace the tired exhausted specimens that now bend against the wind? Perhaps they will go the distance, their reward is to be killed and served as fresh meat to the soldiers whose strength demands it." From what I have seen of the countryside, I cannot remember any tractors in the barnyards. "Are these ordinary farm horses, taken by the army from the fields to serve the state? How can the farmers be expected to provide food for the country if their only means of harvesting is taken from them? It seems like a vicious circle to me. The facts add up to one answer – defeat!"

I must roll over and try to sleep. " Enough of this analyzing the enemy and his food problems. Let them take care of it. What does it matter to me! I'm not getting any of it!"

In the morning, abruptly awakened by shouts from the guards, I feel rested. Sitting up and placing my helmet liner on my head, I think of the day ahead of me. I know what to expect. It is an old story now and all of us are resigned to it. We carry thoughts of escape in our minds continually but until the time presents itself, we must follow this daily routine without question.

"Morning, Jack."

"Morning, Bob."

Rubbing my feet, I notice the feeling is gone from the tips of my toes. Poor circulation from the lack of food and clothing, I guess. A little more rubbing and they feel hot and tingling. A new hole starting in the heel of my stocking catches my attention. "What will I do when they are completely worn out? Surely they wouldn't be replaced from the German supplies." I have heard of using paper around the feet to keep them warm but that wouldn't last very long as a substitute for stockings. Maybe I could fashion a pair from my blanket if I had a needle and thread.

My shoes are like hardened hulks of leather. The constant wading in the snow has soaked them through and the grease I had so carefully applied while at the front lines, is long gone. At night they partially dry from the heat in the room only to turn stiff and hard. Sometimes I think they are more comfortable when wet. At least then they are pliable. Shoving my feet into them, I gently place the worn laces in the proper holes, being careful not to strain them for fear they will break. "Where the hell would I get new shoe laces?"

As we march down the road we can see a woman with a basket on her arm threading her way past the unlighted homes. Snow drifts slow her progress as she follows a rut. Her black knitted shawl covers the lower half of the face and her worn coat is flapping in the wind as if an evil being is trying to hold her back. The wagon train, in passing last night, has left two ruts in the snow filled street.

As we march in two ranks, one in each rut with the guards in front and rear, I wonder if the guards will move aside and let the woman have the right of way in the trail. Most likely they will give her no thought and will brush her aside into the drifts.

I am right. The guards lower their heads as if to shield them against the wind and if the woman hadn't stepped aside they would have knocked her down. As the first prisoner approaches her, he steps off into the snow to pass and the rest of us follow. The guards in the rear stay to the path. We move up the road, each man thinking of the small courtesy he has played a part in and from it comes the warmth of goodness. It lifts our spirits and no doubt will keep them up throughout the day.

The day passes. The night is just another night filled with an aching loneliness.

Again we march away from the schoolhouse, the brisk wind on our faces attesting to the unchanged weather. Cold and stiff, our minds lost in dreams of home, we stumble down the drifted street again following the ruts as if we are walking a tightrope.

There ahead of us comes the lady with the basket. This morning she is holding her head high. Her open shawl reveals a kindly smiling face, with cheeks blushing from the cold wind. As we meet in the trail, she steps aside to let the guards keep the snow off their boots. Then she moves back onto the path.

Our front man in the rank turns to step off the path.

As he does, the man in back of him blocks the rear guards'
view. Her hand opens the lid of the basket to bring within
our reach, apples piled to the brim. She motions for him
to take two, one for himself and one for the man opposite
him. On down the line, each man grasps two apples as if
they are salvation granted from heaven. The last six men
are out of luck as the supply gives out. So covered has
the transaction been that they won't realize until later
what has happened. The guards continue marching with their
heads down, not seeing her at all.

The red apples are hidden in our jackets and shirts
until we can find a place to eat them secretly. As we
reach the barnyard where the wheels and blocks are made,
the left rank detours into it like a pack of dogs following
their master. Jack and I are in the right rank that marches
straight down the street and out into the woods. We follow
the ruts of the oxen wagons to a new location where the
never ending supply of logs awaits us. Care is taken while
lifting the logs to our shoulders not to squash the apples
in our jackets and shirts.

Finally it is noontime. The guards halt the work
and begin preparing their dinner at the wagons. As we
bunch together before sitting down, Jack whispers, "How
about it men, let's keep one apple for the other guys?"
Surprisingly the grunts of approval show the true character
of the men in our group.

"Will all of them keep their word when their stomachs
crave alot more than one apple can provide?" I argue.

Jack answers, "Who knows."

As the guards eat their meal, we sit and watch them
as usual. However, we too have something to eat today.
Suddenly as if by a signal, apples are taken from their
hiding places in unison. The first bite into their frozen
skin hurts our teeth. We smack our lips and chew to get
the fullness of their flavor in our mouth before letting
them slip down to the hungry stomach that awaits.

All eyes are on the guards to see what their reaction
will be. We are eating with hurried slowness because we
want to let the guards see what we have and yet we want
to devour the apples before they can take them away from
us. The reaction is a comedy. Their spoons of hot soup
stop in mid-air before their mouths, cooling to a slimy

91

grease before they recover. There is a short pause and then, all talking at once, they ask one another to explain this mystery.

By this time the apples are gone and so is the courage that made us affront the Germans with such a display of open defiance. Now they are questioning some of the men in the front of the group about the appropriation of the apples. It is a joke to see them feign knowledge of the German language.

After a council, the guards put us back to work. Evidently they have decided they cannot take the time to extract the information from us and therefore they will make us go to work sooner. We are moving more wood today than ever before and I imagine the men in the barnyard are wondering why there is an extra delivery of logs.

When dusk has settled into night we return to the school and enter our room. Pandemonium breaks loose the moment the guards leave. The men with the apples begin to bring the extra ones out of hiding. The would-be receivers are demanding their share of the loot. In a moment it is organized and the apple-less men are given the objects they demand. Peace and quiet again reigns.

Men are huddling in small groups whispering to each other. One telling the other the happenings of the day in the woods while he counters with his description of the barnyard scene where an extra supply of logs have been brought in during the afternoon. Laughter breaks out as Jack acts out the part of a guard with his spoon held motionless before his face and his mouth is agape. It is a happy scene.

Small as the apples are, they have molded this group into a friendly stag party where the drinks are dreams of another apple and the stag motion picture, a delightful remembrance of the looks on the guards faces. We will sleep tonight with a feeling of serenity, creating a long forgotten smile on our lips.

The morning comes too fast, breaking us into our world of stiff knees, sore backs and a gnawing hunger in our stomachs. The events of yesterday are lost in the cold blast of wind smarting our faces. Following the guards out of the school yard into the street, the sight greeting our eyes quickens the pace.

There she is, like an angel of mercy in the dim street. All eyes are glued to the basket we hope contains more apples. With a presence of mind that seems to enter all of us at the same time, we slow our pace to its usual dragging stumble, walking the tight rope as if unexperienced in the proper placement of our feet. The scene is the same as yesterday. The lady steps out of the path for the guards and then steps back as we go around her. Our hands dip into the basket and then to our shirts as if it is an everyday operation. We hope it can be everyday but we know it cannot last. While it does, we are going to make the most of it. As she is met by the last three men, the basket is empty. She steps into the snow to let the rear guards pass.

One rank to the left and one rank to the right as we automatically perform the drill at the barnyard gate. Again a spirit of joy prevails as we plod along with the apples giving off a sort of human warmth generated by our courtesy to the lady with the basket.

The morning work proceeds slowly, for although our minds are all thinking of the coming noon day event, the labor is not eased. Snow covers the stacks of wood making them miserable to handle and slippery to carry. We lug them down the hill, sliding and stopping to regain our foothold.

The oxen are slowly chewing their cuds and blasting streams of frozen air from their nostrils. Their heads droop from the work and the weight of the heavy wooden yoke. They patiently wait for the sting of the whip to signify the load is on and ready to move to the barnyard.

As we trudge back up the steep slope, I grumble, "Why has the wood been stacked on a hill? Why couldn't it have been piled down by the road on the level? It would be alot more convenient."

I don't expect an answer to that question. Our convenience, as far as our work goes, means about as much to the Germans as their concern for the clouds above that are dropping their loads of snow on our heads.

But now at last the noon hour has arrived. The moment is here in all its magnificence. We are thinking of nothing but the juicy succulent apples. The guards take their place as if it is a dress rehearsal for a Broadway play.

We wait for the moment to make our entrance. The scene is set as it was yesterday, only today we know our part to perfection. The spoons are raised and the apples come out as if a cue has been given from the prompter. The guards also know their part well. The looks of astonishment are the same as registered during yesterday's performance.

The munching of the apples breaks the stillness of the woods with a snap as the first bite is taken. It sounds as if all of us have forgotten our table manners and we are chewing with mouths open to get the desired sound effects.

The guards knowing it is a mockery of their authority, lay their spoons and metal soup containers aside. They glare at us with all the contempt a human face can muster. Apples vanish down hungry throats with a speed created only by people who do not want an object taken from them and the only way to stop the act is to put it in a place that cannot be reached.

The smiles on our faces disappear and courage again fades into oblivion. "Have we gone too far in our joke of defiance?" It isn't a joke to the guards. Grabbing their rifles from their resting place against the wagon, they club the nearest men, making them scramble to their feet and start up the hill to work. Obediently and frightened, the rest of us fight to go with them and escape the blows the guards are dealing out to the ones within reach.

The afternoon is prolonged. Our weary bodies are deadened because we have to haul a larger quota of wood to the wagons. The men in the barnyard must know what is happening again when the number of new loads, added to the present supply, stacks high above normal. The unfortunate men, beaten by the guards, fight back the pain as they carry out their share of logs. The rest of us would help them but we know any attempt to do so will bring more blows from the Germans. Our sympathy is conveyed to them as we pass on the hill.

The trip back to Heidweiler is uneventful as every prisoner stays in line and creates a seemingly faster pace up the road. Not one of us wants to provoke another attack.

Excitement boils in the room after the door is shut. The men from the barnyard want to hear all about it and

are feeling sorry for themselves because they missed the
fun. As they hear the full story and see the bruises on
the men who were clubbed, they settle down to a quiet
thoughtfulness and munch on their apples, glad they did
not have to endure the suffering.

Snoring is soon heard from various parts of the room.

"Good night, Bob."

"Good night, Jack."

The wind whistles down the chimney as we close our
eyes and sleep exhausted until morning.

This morning we are not moved out of the schoolyard
right away and I know something is wrong. Accustomed to
the routine for the past weeks, the delay is noticeable.
The Brute is talking to Skinhead and motioning toward us.
Popeye is joining them and now the discussion is split
three ways. The cold is creeping into our feet from the
ankle deep snow but part of the coolness is a growing lack
of knowledge as to what the guards are contemplating.
This is altogether different from anything that has happened
before and although a discussion by the guards is a simple
act, it grows out of proportion in our minds as we recall
yesterday's events.

Calling us to attention with sharp commands, they
proceed between the ranks searching us from shoe tops to
helmet liners. They are looking for lumps beneath our
clothing that will betray the presence of another supply
of apples. Finding none, they start the procession down
the windy street, kicking at the snow with a childlike
hate resulting from defeat in their search. Nervousness
takes over as the lady with the basket again appears through
the whirling snow. The guards know there are no apples
in our possession and if we take them from the basket,
they will soon detect our source of supply.

She steps aside, letting the guards pass, then back
in front of us as we go around her. As the basket is
presented to the first man, his hand reaches out to take
his share. I am fourth in line and know what is happening
in front of me . I quickly shout out:

NO, we'll have NO bananas,
We'll have NO bananas today.

The idea transfers to four other men and they take
up the chorus:

...We'll have NO bananas today.

The interruption of the usual silence so startles the man whose hand is reaching for the apples that he pauses for an instant. That is enough. I make myself stumble against the man in front of me and the action carries forward against the man in front of him until the first man is pushed past the basket. He is unable to grab a single apple.

The lady with the basket knows something is happening to stop her secret act and she quickly covers the apples.

At noon the guards scrutinize our faces for some sign that we may try more tricks while they eat. They are openly disappointed as they pass a dull noon hour with nothing to do but eat. They watch us every minute and we feel almost as defiant as the day before because they expect us to do something and we cannot be moved into any provoking act. Jack has a smile on his face as we again trudge up the hill. "It's the little things in life that count," he jokes.

"Yeah," I agree, "like their minds." That brings a quiet laugh as we each bend down to pick up a log. The afternoon wears on and our quota is not raised. The guards are almost jovial again in their actions and remarks. They believe they have subdued us to their will.

At last the day is over and the night's shadows creep across the clearing of our work area. The last load starts with the crack of a whip as we follow down the valley. Joining us at the barnyard, the other men complete the procession to the school. We are halted and searched again. Evidently they think we might have picked up some apples on the way home. Finding none, they turn us loose in our room. With the door shut, the room again fills with laughter. By doing nothing to aggravate the guards during the day we have created as much of a disturbance as yesterday.

Now something new has come into our lives. We have a new thought to occupy our minds. "What will we do tomorrow? Better let the guards forget our boldness before we try anything else. They have the power to subdue us and will delight in using it if we push them too far."

As we eat our bread, Jack suggests, "Why don't we save our nourishment for morning? Won't the bread do us

96

more good by eating it before we go to work in the morning than before we go to sleep at night?"

"Too late now," I reply, "but we can try it starting tomorrow."

We talk of escape as we lie on the blanket waiting for sleep to possess us.

"It has to be a sure thing before we try it," Jack stipulates. "If they catch us it will be our lives."

Plans of getting on the work detail in the barnyard and hiding until the day is over, later to come out and run, are rejected.

"The guards are with us almost every minute, except when we unload the chips in the barn. Then they wait outside knowing there is no exit except the big doors where they stand. If four go in, four have to come out," I establish by expressing the facts. "It's difficult to plan an escape in such a small group where we will be missed in just a few minutes."

"Yeah. Guess we'll have to think of some other way," Jack muses.

He fishes a "toothbrush" from his shirt pocket. It is a piece of willow stick four inches long, slit at one end many times and when soaked in water, it fans out to form tiny bristles. Crude but fashionable in our group.

Tonight my eyes are heavy and burning from the glare of today's fresh snowfall. It has been snowing for a week. At least it is warmer when it snows. I wonder what the temperature is. Probably below zero. My feet tingle under the cover of my field jacket. Every night I cover them hoping they will work up a little circulation from the heat. The numbness now engulfs my toes to where they join my foot and they itch when the warm jacket is laid on them.

The results of a discussion breaks into our privacy as one man calls for silence in the room. Acting as a spokesman for the small group, he is recounting, "Men, we were lucky today. If we had taken any apples our lives might have been jeopardized, to say nothing of the lady with the basket."

He shifts his weight to the other foot as if not accustomed to commanding such an attentive group and then continues, "We've got a problem now that must be discussed. Should we take the apples tomorrow if they are offered?"

97

"Not if we are searched," a voice rasps, "otherwise why not? Only let's not defy them at noontime by eating them as we did yesterday."

I locate the man who is speaking. He is a nondescript man in this group where the order of the day is shaggy beards, long hair, torn shirts matched with dirty sleeves and wrinkled pants stuck into water soaked shoes.

I tap Jack's shoulder to get his attention, whispering, "History is being written in this group. It's the first attempt to organize and he is the first one to address the chair."

Jack replies, "Yes, and it will pass into the night with no one to record its birth."

A vote is taken and the consensus of opinion is that we take the apples if they are offered tomorrow. We, however, will not show them and only when we reach our room at night will we eat them. Everyone agrees.

Chapter Seven

The gruff voice of The Brute starts us stirring in the morning. He seems to derive joy from waking us for another day of hard labor.

Jack looks over at me and smiles, "He must eat nails for breakfast." We enjoy a short laugh as we don our helmet liners.

"Quite a piece of equipment," I remark as I adjust the strap under my chin. "Wash bowl, pillow, stool and head gear all wrapped into one tough piece of plastic. How can so light a product be so damn tough?" I ask as we prepare to file down the stairs.

Two of the men, beaten the day before in the woods, are in bad shape. Pain racks their heads where the rifle butts struck. One of them is Joker. He has a gash behind his ear. The lump under the laceration will not let it heal. His shirt collar shows bloodstains from the trickle of blood that flowed during the night. His eyes are bloodshot and matter forms at the corners. The other man, though not as badly beaten, takes up a look of misery to match his friend's. The rifle butt just grazed his head and struck his shoulder. It pains him to move and his arm hangs lifeless.

The Polish guard with the limp enters to clear the room. He stops short when he sees Joker and his friend still lying in their places. Going over to them, he shouts, "Raus! Raus!"

They look up at him with expressions of anguish on their faces. Not moving, they try to explain their painful physical condition and suggest with a pleading voice that they be allowed to remain in the room for the day.

He looks them over carefully as he drags them to their feet. Seeing the gash and the drooping shoulder, he grunts, pushes them aside and leaves the room.

In a minute we can hear voices raised in argument; one in Polish, one in German.

Popeye enters our room led by the Polish guard. He gives the men one quick look and then nods his head. The two injured prisoners are to be left in the room guarded by the Pollack.

The line up at the faucet moves slowly. Finally we get in formation in front of the school.

It seems warmer this morning as if the sun is in a hurry to show its light for the day. The air is brisk and makes each sound echo as we wait to be led out of the yard. A far off rooster crows a cheery welcome to the warmer weather.

"Why doesn't he stay in his coop where he can still sleep?" I grumble.

"Yeah," Jack complains, "we have to get up. But not because we want to wish anyone a good morning."

With an air of commanding an entire division The Brute gives us the word to move out.

"God, what a mind for devilish thoughts this man has!" I begin to agree with Jack about the "breakfast of nails."

The street has been plowed!

"How did they do that?" I muse. "I didn't hear a truck pass. Maybe I slept too soundly last night?"

It is much easier walking this morning and we no longer have to place one foot directly ahead of the other. The snow crunches under our shoes, echoing between the houses.

Farther down the street appears the lady and she has her basket. She steps into the road, stops momentarily and surveys the plowed wideness before her. She walks along slowly, pondering her next move. Now she proceeds a few steps toward us, then stops again. Fifty yards separate us and we are closing the gap fast. Turning, she starts back toward her home.

Suddenly she whirls about, her head is held high, her chin jutting forward. There is a stately look about her squared shoulders. The grandeur of determination glows in her face. She cannot know the displeasure her apples have already caused the guards. I feel as though the very sight of an apple will throw them into another fit of anger. Surely she cannot cross this plowed expanse and supply us with apples without being detected! If the guards find out our source, she will be in great danger.

She is on the far side of the road fifteen yards in front of us. Looking neither left nor right, she strides forward as if she hasn't seen the group of men ahead of her.

As she nears, I cannot help but think of the risk she took while passing apples to us the past few days. Even though expertly covered in her act, it was one of

100

great daring. Her life was at stake every time a man reached into her basket. If she had been caught, They might have shot her for aiding prisoners of war.

"What reasoning traveled through her brain each morning as she filled her basket, knowing its purpose and the risk it involved? Was it all because of the small courtesy shown her by our men after the guards had pushed her into the snow to stand while they passed? Was it because she felt sorry for the men she saw, thin faced, tired and obviously hungry? Or could it be the fact that she would show the German State she had a mind of her own; one that is filled with decency and thought for human feelings?"

"Was she trying to convey the feeling of the German civilians, held in terror by these men who are trained to mete out animal-like treatment to all who are against them? Are they also prisoners like us? Their lives guarded and watched to see if they act for the good of Germany? Maybe there are decent people here after all"! The idea shocks me. I have always thought of them as enemies.

She is almost parallel with the first guard. I watch as her hand fumbles with the basket cover. Suddenly she stumbles and apples are rolling into our ranks like bowling balls. We snatch them up quickly, breaking rank to reach those that stop short of us. In an instant they are all retrieved. She is struggling to her feet, not an obstacle around to make her trip and fall.

I think, "Is this what she planned when she stopped in front of her house while looking at the plowed street? If so, then that explains her sudden look of determination and her squared shoulders when she whirled about. That makes her walk of fifty yards to meet us the same as a martyr stepping to the hangman's noose."

Rifles come off the shoulders of the guards as they rush to her. They have seen the apples and instantly know our source. They crowd around her, leaving us to hungrily eat the apples.

While we stand unguarded, watching the scene with anxiety, the guards fire questions at her, all speaking at once and expecting an answer to each individual question. She briskly brushes the snow from her threadbare coat, holding onto her basket as though it is a part of her life.

It is a part of her life now, a major turning point that can spell death if she cannot control these infuriated men before her.

She speaks, slowly and with determination, pointing to a spot on the road that is as smooth as a table. Our interpreter informs us that she is telling them she has tripped on something in the road. The inflection in her voice makes me think a huge rock was blocking her path and in a crawling over it, she fell, strewing apples under our feet.

"How will she ever get out of the spot she is in now?" I ask Jack.

He shakes his head, the motion telling me to be quiet so he can listen to them, although I know he cannot understand a word they are saying.

Suddenly she points to us, her outstretched arm shaking as she shrieks at the guards for their laxity in letting us eat up all her fruit.

It is amazing to see the guards step back in astonishment. They are sure she has spilled them on purpose. They are also sure they have found the source of our past supply even if they are unable to determine the way we received them. Instead of apologizing for her act she has turned on them, pointing out that it is all their fault. The idea is so quickly planted in their muddled heads that they believe it and turn back to us.

We are, for the moment, grateful to see the guards come at us, not caring for ourselves but glad to see her proceed down the street. We can see the smile on her face as she passes. We quickly form two ranks and march down the street as the guards reach us. They fall in line and are carried along, their minds still in a whirl. Not a word is said about the vanished apples. The repercussions we expect have lost their momentum.

The barnyard is reached without further interruption and the left rank files into it without a command. All is quiet and orderly. The rest of us proceed to the woods

We follow the newly made oxen tracks to our day's supply of logs, where the men will perform their work with perfection to soothe the guards.

Noontime passes without incident.

At about three o'clock we hear a roaring noise. The

sky is clear. The deep rumbling sound is almost upon us. The guards realizing some planes are approaching, halt our work and instruct us to stand perfectly still under the trees.

The sounds come from behind the hill and we watch four American planes zoom over our heads, their machine guns sounding like a snare drum, sharp and fast. The pilots zero in on two of the ox wagons that are on the road to town, thinking them to be part of another supply train.

Our position on the hillside gives us an excellent view of the fields and town.

The wagon drivers are fleeing to the wooded hills like scared rabbits before the attack. The oxen, frightened by the hellish noise, stampede down the road with their load careening after them. Bullets find their marks and one ox stumbles and falls, bellowing in pain. His mate is pulled down with him and the load of logs crashes into them, spilling its contents on their thrashing bodies. They lay quiet now; their blood soaking the snow crimson red.

The other wagon has met a similar fate and one ox is struggling to free himself from the harness that is binding him to his dead mate. His hooves are pawing the snow with a fierceness that reveals the panic in his frightened brain.

The planes zoom over the town and circle to the left, coming around the hill for a second pass. They roar over us, heading for their next target. Then the bombs leave their nest under the wings and plummet toward the earth, exploding in a section of barns like a giant firecracker. Roofs and walls fall apart revealing a convoy of supply trucks hiding beneath them.

The pilots must have spotted the tire trails cut deep into the road in front of the barns and they immediately know what story they told. Again the planes circle left, their machine guns stuttering a steady stream of incendiary bullets into the dried remains of the barns. Those that have not burst into flames from the bombs, now catch fire and the scene is one of utter destruction.

Once again the planes turn and fan out across the village, searching for another target they may have missed. Finding none, they angle up and out of sight, vanishing over the hill behind us as if they want to leave the same way they entered.

We can only stand here in awe and look at the destruction spread in the last few minutes. There are no cheers from the prisoners.

I try to collect my thoughts and wonder how this latest development of the day will affect us.

I can see the oxen sprawling in the snow. One is still living and has partially freed himself from the broken harness. Through sheer power from fright he is turning the upset wagon sideways as he crawls from beneath its load. The others lie still, their working days are finished.

"Bob," Jack calls to me. As I walk toward him, he chimes out, "Beautiful isn't it!" A smile automatically forms on his face as he derives pleasure from the bombings.

"Don't let them know you think so," I challenge.

Picking up a log, I start down the hill careful to avert the guards' eyes as I pass.

The road is blocked by the two broken wagons and so we load the other wagons and move in a body down to the sight to clear them. Soon the spilled logs are repiled alongside the road and teams of oxen are hooked onto the dead animals, pulling them off to the side. Now we can pass with the loaded wagons and proceed into town.

The guards are anxious to see the damage and try to salvage what they can.

Jack and I are walking shoulder to shoulder. "That's why the road is plowed, to let the supply convoy through," I murmur in undertones so as not to aggravate the guards. Inwardly I have to laugh to myself, "Our fly boys have put an end to that supply convoy."

We are led straight up the road where the prisoners from the barnyard join us. Popeye and one Polish guard lead the group to the school. The rest of the guards go directly to the scene of the bombing.

As I seat myself on the floor, my back against the wall underneath the window, Jack is stirring up the fire in the stove. The small branches we carried in will heat the room until morning.

He sits next to me and starts to talk about the day's events. "I can't imagine them letting the lady with the

104

apples get away with her actions today."

"Maybe after they think it over, they may still go after her," I suggest.

"They will have a hard time proving she stumbled on purpose, though," he continues.

"They don't have to prove anything," I laugh. "All they have to do is make up their minds as to what they should do and proceed to do it, that's all."

Jack pauses thinking deeply. "You know what?" he declares while turning to me, "She should be awarded a medal for what she did. It took alot of courage. And she didn't have anything to gain by it except peace in her own mind."

"Well, what about those planes today? The pilots should get a medal for their actions too. Wasn't it something to see! Scared the hell out of me as they came in low over our ringside seats but I enjoyed every minute of it."

Jack laughs, "Yes, but if you think you were scared, you should have been watching Eightball. He looked like a two year old kid trying to hide under a bare branch of a four inch sapling. He was right below me and as he looked over his shoulder to watch the planes come in, his eyes were sticking out of his head so far I could have knocked them off with a snowball! I'll bet he'll have to change his underwear tonight!" Now we're both laughing as we visualize the scene.

"I don't imagine it will improve the guards' tempers though," he mumbles. "I wonder what effect it will have on our living conditions?"

"Well, for one thing, they can't take away anything we haven't got and we sure don't have much, do we?"

"No, but I'm sure The Brute will think of something in short order if he puts his mind to it."

"Say, do you realize it's still daylight out and here we are home already? It's the shortest day I've put in since we arrived at this swell Stalag."

It almost seems impossible to be able to sit here and talk for awhile without being so tired. Leaning forward I carefully unlace my soaked shoes. "Do you realize this is the most I've talked since we arrived here! Before I didn't have much chance for conversation. Roger's throat was so sore he couldn't talk."

Looking up I ask myself, "I wonder where he is now?"

Jack can read my thoughts and he puts his hand on my shoulder, "Don't worry about Roger. He's O.K. I'm sure he wouldn't want you to feel sorry for him," he consoles. "For all you know he's probably in some hospital getting fat with four nurses waiting on him."

As he laughs over his own joke, he turns my thoughts back to untying my knotted laces. They resist my efforts but finally I can slip the shoes from my feet. It makes a sound like a cow pulling her foot out of the mud. My socks cling to my feet, sticking there as if they are a part of the skin. I roll them off and gently wring them out, afraid to twist too hard for fear of tearing them.

My feet are white and wrinkled from the day long soaking. "Ugly things," I grunt as I dry them with the blanket. "You know, Jack, wool doesn't absorb water very well but the friction makes my toes prick and itch as the circulation tries to reach them. Funny thing about them, lately the numbness is slowly creeping farther back into my feet. It's half way to my heel now."

"Mine, too," he replies.

Covering my legs with my field jacket and sitting up straight again, I glance over at Jack. "What a hell of a life we're leading!"

His smile breaks out as he answers, "Yes, not much chance for a promotion here, is there?" We laugh again. Then my mind wanders.

I am glad I have met Jack. Our companionship throughout the past few days seems to have lightened a burden on both our shoulders. It feels good to again know that I have a friend I can depend on. Funny thing, it seems as though I have known him all of my life and yet it is only a week.

Jack reminds me, "Tonight is the night we start saving our bread until morning, you know, and it shouldn't be too hard because of the easy day we had."

The thought passes through my mind. "What difference can a slice of bread make to my stomach whether it gets it tonight or tomorrow? After I have stopped swallowing, it still growls for more!"

Two days ago I finished the loaf of bread in my bread sack. Jack wouldn't take any. I tried to convince him

106

it would be alright but he refused. I wanted to make it last longer but the idea of having it and not eating it was too great a temptation. I nibbled on it every chance I had and it disappeared in a hurry. It only made my hunger increase as my stomach had shrunk for lack of food and now it seems to want more since it has felt full for the first time in weeks. The apples have fulfilled its demand the past few days but now to think of not eating my bread tonight makes it groan in despair.

"God, I'm sleepy."

Unconsciously I close my eyes as I slide to the floor to be more comfortable. Jack sits alongside me brushing his teeth.

"Guess I'll have to get a new toothbrush at the PX tomorrow," he jokes.

A smile turns up the corner of my mouth as I fall off the precipice into sleep. Visions of home appear in my mind and the table laden with food seems so real, I can smell the beef roast. My mother is scurrying around the room getting things ready before calling us four boys to eat. After the grace, I fill my plate with roast beef, mashed potatoes, lettuce salad, peas and carrots and fresh home baked bread. Just as I raise my fork loaded with potatoes and gravy, my dream is ruined. The Brute has opened our prison door.

"ACH-TUNG." he shouts, jolting me right out of my first good meal in 1945. Standing there, feet apart, shaking his fist at us, his voice is filling the room with German words unknown to me. He leaves after his short tirade.

The interpreter informs us that because of the planes bombing the village, we will not receive our bread ration tonight.

"Well, Jack ol' buddy, it doesn't look like we will be able to try out our new plan of saving the bread tonight?"

"No," he agrees, "I guess they're pretty well teed off at the way our planes put the boots to their supply convoy." He pauses then continues, "What do they think war is anyway? When they are winning it is O.K. but now they expect the Allies to handle their country with kid gloves. They'll wish they hadn't started this war when we get through with them." Another pause, "Of course, they will be surly until the end. I wonder what kind of treatment they'll expect when they're defeated? Probably cry like hell if they don't get three square meals a day. And they won't want to work for it either!"

"Yeah, and the world will demand we give it to them!" I add. "If we try to give them a taste of their own medicine we would be called barbarians."

"They'll never be put on trail before the world for this."

"Maybe a few of the bigshots will but how about men like The Brute who delights in seeing us wallow in our own filth and starving us beyond human limits? He actually enjoys beating the men and showing off his brute strength before us. What about him? He will never have to pay for it — unless he is still with is when we are liberated."

"If he is, I'll bet the men will kill him."

"God help him if he asks for mercy."

"The men would probably spit in his face and ask him how he likes it. I know our religious training will be forgotten then, just when we should forgive him."

"Do you think we could control the mob, Jack?"

He shrugs his shoulders, "I don't know. I don't know if he even deserves it and yet the Bible tells us he does. I guess all we can do now is think of ourselves and take care of other things as we come to them. One thing I do know and that is if he heard the things we just said, he really would raise hell. I don't think he will ever concede defeat and be taken prisoner. Surely it hasn't entered his mind because any sane man would immediately change his ways if he thought soon his prisoners would be his jailers."

"That part is true except for one thing," I point out.

"What's that?" he questions.

"He isn't a sane man!"

Chapter Eight

"Rise and shine," Jack pronounces as he shakes my shoulder. "I hear movement in the guards' room and they'll be in to wake us in a minute. If we get our shoes on now we won't be late in getting out of the room in case their tempers are still hot. The last few prisoners may be helped out, you know."

I'm sure he is right but I hate to move. It's so much easier just to lie here and sleepily rub my eyes. "I wonder if I'll ever get a chance to catch up on sleep?" I mutter. "Someday I'm going to sleep the clock around."

"Good enough," he jokes, "but right now you better get moving or you'll never see that day."

The door flies open and Popeye comes through the doorway as if he isn't going to stop until he hits the opposite wall. He isn't fully dressed yet. His suspenders are hanging at the sides of his pants and the top of his dirty underwear is unbuttoned. He has his socks on but no shoes. He looks like a clown standing there trying to see us out of his one good eye that I just noticed is crossed. The ever faithful pipe is missing also. He shouts a few words in German and although we cannot understand him, we know he isn't telling us we can go back to sleep.

A moment of fright holds the group motionless at the foot of the stairs. The gloating eyes of the silent guards survey the mass of disheveled men. Stacked neatly in the middle of the yard is a supply of shovels and picks. We have heard of men having to dig their own graves and that thought crosses our minds. The guards may have been tormented past the point of reason by yesterday's bombings and now they may want to be rid of us.

Stepping out into the schoolyard seems an arduous task as every man's gaze freezes on the tools.

"Would these maniacs actually go through with it?" I ask myself. Silently I pray to God to spare us.

We march over to the tools and are told to pick them up. Men's arms reach for the handles that we do not want to grasp. They lay heavy and cumbersome on our shoulders as we march down the road. The left rank is not detoured into the barnyard and at the next intersection we turn right, down a narrow side street. Suddenly my despair turns to delight as I realize we are marching in the direction of the bombed supply trucks.

Reaching the area, our eyes record the damage. The trucks have been hiding in a semi-circle of barns. Evidently some prosperous German official owns this estate and had a group of families working for him. The herd of cattle, long ago eaten by the German Army, had been housed in these fine high roofed barns. On one side, a group of vacant two room houses, now partially burned, stands out against the high stone wall that surrounds the yard.

Broken wagons, left as useless by earlier convoys, dot the landscape. Parts of trucks and broken boards litter the area and I cannot see one whole truck that has escaped the bombs or fire. They are a total loss, although some of their loads seem to be intact.

The Germans have not been able to make much progress except to control the fires. The barns are gutted. They stand like ghosts against the background of the hills. Four barns are completely demolished, their walls and roofs caved in, scattered into a mingling jig-saw. Bomb craters, like the inside of huge volcanoes, look up at the sky as if to swallow any more objects that might fall from the blasted buildings.

Our job is to clear the heaping rubble and fill the holes! We start the job with relief in our minds.

The boards are to be separated from the broken walls and piled on one side. Broken tile from the roofs have to be sorted and any good pieces kept for later use. The scrap is thrown into the bomb craters to bring them level with the rest of the yard. Dirt has been heaved onto the debris by the explosions. Our shovels are useless because of the boards, cement and tile that are mixed in the pile. We dig at them with our freezing bare hands, pulling and prying the debris loose.

After a morning's labor the courtyard looks unchanged. We survey it from our seats on the ground while watching the guards eat. It gives us a chance to warm our hands by rubbing them in our hair.

How I envy the guards as they slurp their way through steaming pots of hot soup. They are talking among themselves without a glance in our direction, wiping their greasy lips on their coat sleeves. Later, lighting up cigarettes, they lean back against an overturned wagon puffing and enjoying life as if they have just dined at the Chez Paree.

Turning to Jack, I mutter, "They remind me of so many pigs, stretching out to rest after filling their guts from a trough."

Chipmunk, the one with buckteeth, pulls an apple from his lunch bucket and as he starts to bite into it, I envision an imaginary snow fence between his teeth and the apple.

"Yep," I confirm out loud, "I believe he could."

Jack looks at me questioning my statement. "Could what?"

"Eat an apple through a snow fence with those two buckteeth."

The men within hearing distance break into laughter as they look at Chipmunk. This brings a glare on the guards' faces as they turn to see what has caused the eruption. Seeing nothing amiss they return to their own private discussions.

The prisoner sitting next to Jack turns to him and volunteers, "You know what I think they were hauling in those trucks?"

"No, what?"

"Red Cross food parcels for prisoners of war. I saw the markings on the cartons."

We are thunderstruck by the news! Those parcels are meant for us but they are hauling them to THEIR front line troops! If they had intended to give them to us, we would have received them yesterday. Satisfied with my deductions, I ponder, "If only they will let us clean up those barns where the trucks are, maybe some of their loads are still salvageable. Somehow we might manage to get our hands on a few separated articles and perhaps find it good enough to eat."

The rumor of the Red Cross food parcels spreads through the prisoners with speed. Heads are put together as men speculate as to what the parcels contain. The thought of food conjures up dreams of meat, dehydrated eggs and milk, coffee and a host of other items. The guards are soon forgotten and the buzzing of voices grows to outbreaks of laughter.

"Raus! Raus!" brings us to our feet as the guards enter the dream. Not knowing what has brought on the disturbance, they will not let us enjoy our moment of joy any longer.

The pile of rubble resists our efforts for the rest of the afternoon as we work to clear the area. Each man has a dream of his own by now as to what the packages contain.

The guards, seeing us work harder, think we are finally beginning to admit defeat to their will and when a heavy object is encountered they pitch in to help. They are helping us closer to our ultimate goal and we, not caring what the reason is, welcome their strong backs.

As Jack and I carry a heavy timber to the growing pile of salvage, he observes, "I sure hope none of the guys goof off now and let the guards in on our secret."

"That would really fix him with the rest of us if he does," I concur.

We have no control over what the men will do and we can only pray they will not, by some action, signal the Germans as to what we are working for. This idea enters the minds of the other men as we work and an air of submission prevails with each man darting side glances at the next, trying to pierce his mind and see if he will be the one.

In a short while the men are working with a frenzy. Tile and boards are being carried to their respective piles with a speed that will soon alert the guards that something besides their presence is pushing us faster. Something has to be done! Someone has to stop this growing threat of too much speed which is unlike our usual pace.

Now The Brute is talking to Popeye and glancing in the direction of the prisoners who are upset by this sudden change in attitude.

A few minutes ago we were dreaming about food that will give us a new strength and now we can see it slipping from our grasp because of our anxiety. The very thought of food to starving men can make them do unbelievable things. It seems incredible, however, that we may do something that will keep us from obtaining that same food. Yet if nothing is done, the chance to get some food will be gone.

112

The guards are sensing the tension in the air. It seems an explosive situation with nourishment just a few feet away. We are going to muff it if we do not control our actions.

Jack bends near me and hisses, "Do something!"

"What can I do?"

"Start singing! Dance! Anything! But do something!" he demands.

Roll me over, in the clover,
Roll me over, lay me down and do it again...

I don't know if it's the relief from the stillness that breaks the tension or the sound of my hoarse voice that stirs these men to their senses, but the air is filled with raspy voices as we sing a song familiar to us.

Oh, this is number one, And my song has just begun,
Roll me over, lay me down and do it again.
Roll me over, in the clover,
Roll me over, lay me down and do it again.

Oh, this is number two, and my hand is on her shoe,
Roll me over, lay me down and do it again.
Roll me over, in the clover,
Roll me over, lay me down and do it again.

The guards let us finish the ten verses.

Work progresses as before. The men are calm and with their thoughts collected, they proceed to look like prisoners of war who have nothing to gain by working hard.

The sun is slowly disappearing behind the courtyard wall. Soon the day will be over and we will retire to our privacy in the schoolroom to discuss the situation. It is obvious to all of us that some sort of planned pilfering must be arranged or else the deal will end up a calamity.

Skinhead is struggling to lift one end of a huge center beam as two prisoners pry on the levers beneath it. The beam refuses to budge and The Brute strolls over to watch, a smile on his face. He knows his assistance will be wanted but he won't volunteer it.

As Skinhead grunts under the load, the beam moves a few inches. The Brute, seeing his chances fading to

113

show off in front of the others, steps forward and puts his shoulder to the task. Spouting orders to the men with the levers and placing his feet wide apart, he starts to lift.

The men with the levers look as though they are straining against the poles but at a closer glance I can see it is just a sham with no power applied.

The full weight of the beam now rests on the two guards. On their faces, signs of frustration show they are weakening. Popeye joins them and the three of them now grunt and groan without results.

By this time the men in the other work details have their eyes glued to the scene. Secretly laughing to themselves, they turn back to their jobs and will not offer to help.

The Brute's eyes are bulging, his muscles straining to their utmost. His heavy coat unbuttons without assistance as he shifts his position. His package of cigarettes falls to the ground unnoticed by him.

Three prisoners jump to his assistance and though they help him move the beam, they also relieve him of some cigarettes.

In the shuffle the other guards miss this act of stealing. The package of cigarettes is picked up and dropped again in a flash. It is done with a dexterity by hands that know if they are caught it will mean trouble with The Brute. Now he buttons his coat and in looking down, notices the package of cigarettes at his feet. Bending over, he picks it up and jams it back in its proper pocket without feeling the flatness of the pack.

Popeye and Skinhead are wiping the sweat from their foreheads. The look on their faces as they glance at The Brute is one of victory over his well talked about strength. He has tried to show what weaklings they are and in doing so has failed miserably.

Turning around and retrieving his rifle from one of the Polish guards, The Brute is deep in thought. His head hangs down as he adjusts the firearm on his shoulder. It evidently irritates him because he switches it from the shoulder he had used to lift the beam and cradles it in his other arm.

Searching the group of prisoners for the interpreter,

The Brute gargles a few words in German at him. His voice sounds soft and without its usual gutteral tones. It's as if he is trying to soften the blow to his ego and the interpreter explains that as soon as one more bomb crater is filled, we can start for "home."

Thirty-nine men drop their present job and rush to the smallest hole.

Seeing this, The Brute takes a step toward us to detour the stream of men to a larger hole. He stops after a few steps and stands there. He knows it will defeat his purpose if he gets hard-boiled again. Shaking his head as if to put off the laugh that is starting up in his throat, he looks at Eightball and breaks into loud guffaws, slapping his knee and enjoying the trick that has just been played on him.

With all the shovels concentrating on one spot, the hole is filled quickly. Keeping his word, The Brute starts us through the gate and down the road toward "home."

Jack and I are at the end of the line as we march down the road. He reflects, "This looks like a show I saw one time, 'Snow White and the Seven Dwarfs.' Looks just like us marching home from work with shovels and picks swinging over our shoulders with no thought of keeping in step." He can always make a joke out of any situation and I admire him for it.

We enter the schoolroom after the usual congestion at the doorway. It happens this way every night without fail and no one tries to correct it. There should be no rush to get into the room because nothing special awaits us there, nevertheless every man crowds up the stairs and shoves his way into the room.

We go over to our places like horses knowing which stall we belong in. One by one we slide to the floor and stretch out. Grunts and groans fill the room as we ease our aching muscles. The plaster walls echo back our words as if to tell us that they too are a part of the German State and resent our voicing our opinion of the day's work. In a few minutes snores break through the chattering as a few men, too exhausted to stay awake for their ration of bread, fall asleep on the hardwood floor.

A loud, "Well, I'll be damned!" gains our attention and the humming voices stop as three men stand up. We watch as they examine something in the hand of the one who has let loose the exclamation. He steps forward and is holding up five small white objects. Not having feasted our eyes on so many cigarettes at one time for months, we fail to recognize them.

"Men, those trucks MUST hold Red Cross Parcels! These are Lucky Strikes! The guards were working on them yesterday and must have a pretty good supply for themselves by now."

We crowd around him as he holds them up for display. The sight is unbelievable to us who have stopped smoking through no effort of our own. Five whole cigarettes! American cigarettes! Perfectly round and smooth, waiting for a match to send them curling up in smoke.

The door is pushed open as The Brute announces our dinner, "Brot! Brot!"

The cigarettes are quickly pulled down from sight and hidden in the owner's pocket. Bread is passed around and the sleeping men are awakened to get their share. One slice of hard sour bread to feed our growling stomachs. Small as it is, we welcome it as if it is a seven course meal.

Tonight is the night Jack and I plan to save our bread until morning. It's going to be difficult but once we get over the temptation to attack it in our hunger, we will manage to save it. I mention this to Jack as we head for our spot on the floor.

He smiles and responds, "It won't be quite as hard as you think."

I wonder what he means.

While I'm thinking about it I stumble over my helmet liner on the floor and bump against the wall. My bread breaks in two and I quickly kneel to retrieve the crumbs.

Jack laughs at me sweeping the floor with the side of my hand as I try to get all of it corralled.

Paying no attention to him, I proceed to scoop up every crumb, which I automatically toss into my mouth. "Can't take a chance on losing those crumbs so I had to eat them!" I find myself defensively apologizing.

A guilty look comes over my face as I realize that I have already started eating what I said I was going to save for the morning. "I didn't know where to put..."

"I know, I know," Jacks kids me, a broad smile again showing his white teeth.

"By the way, what did you mean when you said it won't be so hard to save our bread till morning?"

"This," Jack discloses as he pulls an apple from under his shirt.

My look of astonishment rushes him into an explanation.

"I saved this out of the ones we picked up in the street. You know, the ones spilled by the lady. I had it last night and I was going to use it to help us start on this new plan of ours. I knew it would be hard not to eat our bread once we had it in our hands so I saved this to take our minds off of it. When we didn't get our bread last night, I figured everyone else was in the same fix we were and if they could stand it so could we."

I can see the light of his thinking and I'm proud of him. He might have saved it for himself but that would be beyond our friendship.

When we joined forces he said we would share everything and he meant it. Reaching over, I muss up his healthy head of hair and agree, "You take the cake, Jack."

Placing the apple on the floor, Jack places his left forefinger across the top of it and strikes it with the side of his right fist. The apple splits neatly and he hands me my half. We lean back against the wall and slowly eat our dinner.

The man with the cigarettes stands up again and calls for attention.

"Men, we know what is in those packages on the trucks now and we must plan a way to get a share of it without being seen. While we are trying to think this out, if you will get together in groups of eight, I'll pass out the cigarettes and we can split them."

Confusion spreads as we hustle to join in the treat.

Still standing, the man continues, "We first should choose someone to run this meeting." He looks around for volunteers. "I suggest we get a leader and make plans because of the danger involved in stealing food from the Germans."

Jack pipes up, "Any man that will share these cigarettes with the whole bunch like you're doing is good enough to run the show. You got my vote."

Though we are busy taking turns puffing on the cigarettes, everyone agrees with Jack and the newly elected leader thanks us for our confidence.

As he stands in front of this group of eager men, I try to "character read" him. He is almost six feet tall and I guess his normal weight should be about one hundred and eighty pounds. After being a prisoner for almost two months, he looks like he weighs about one hundred and thirty. Light brown hair blossoms out from his head in a semi-pompadore. His hair, like ours, is so long that it now curls over his ears and completely covers the back of his neck. His wind burned face has a trace of wrinkles showing through the beard. An intelligent face, it gives off a radiance of friendly light. His clothes are in the same shape as the rest of ours: dirty, wrinkled and torn from the work we have been doing. His voice, soft and clear, breaks through my thoughts as he asks for suggestions on how to proceed in the forthcoming stealing operation.

"Does anyone have any ideas on how we should go about securing some food from the trucks without the guards catching us? Remember, if we are caught it will go bad for us."

From the far side of the room comes a small voice, timid in its suggestion, "Don't you think we should take a vote to see if all of us want to take the risk of stealing from them?"

"A good idea. All in favor of going ahead with making plans, signify by the usual sign."

A roar of "Ayes" answer his question.

"Any against?"

Thirty-eight heads turn toward the man who had made the suggestion. There are no votes to the negative.

Going on with the meeting, the chair asks for suggestions again. Men start voicing their opinions to their partners in whispers and none volunteer them to the group as a whole.

"Come on, men, let's speak up and make known some of these great plans," he persuades with deliberate flattery, knowing their reluctance.

A tall redhead in the middle of the group speaks, "It's a sure thing that we all can't just go ahead on our own and try to take things."

The timid voice again adds, "How do we know that we will even get a chance to work on the trucks?"

A low muttering emits from the men as they look at him.

The leader states in a smooth voice, "I think we will because otherwise they would have been unloaded already by the Germans." This seems to quiet the man and so we aggain turn to the immediate problem.

"I don't know if we will get at it tomorrow or not but if we do, a plan made tonight will be in our best interest," the leader explains. All this time Jack has been quiet in his own thoughts.

Getting to his feet, Jack speaks with a slow drawl, "Well now, I've been thinking it over and although it isn't clear yet, it seems to me that it would be better if just so many men are designated to take the food and the rest cover for them. Of course, the men who take the food will have to volunteer because of the risk involved. I also think we will start working on it tomorrow because the Germans know the food will be ruined if it is left where it is now."

The leader injects, "Sounds good so far."

Jack continues, "The job of carrying it to the place where it will be stored won't take as long as the time it will take to gather it from the trucks because of the condition the boxes are in. It will have to be sorted and picked over to see what is salvageable and what is not. That means there will be a jam up of men at the trucks, which is just what we want. It will create a little diversion for the guards if a small scuffle or a few jokes are going on at that time. The guards will unconsciously turn toward them and that is the time when the articles must be hidden in the takers pockets. They, of course, will be completely covered by the other men and away from the jokes or scuffles." Jack sits down acting embarrassed over making such a long speech.

His ideas make sense to the rest of us and now every man is talking about how to create a disturbance to draw the guards' attention.

The leader holds up his hand, commanding, "Quiet!" As a smile crosses his face, he speaks, "I don't think this group needs to make plans for a diversion. All you

119

have to do is act normal and let your actions bring up something on the spur of the moment and it will be sufficient." We join him in a round of laughter.

Again the timid voice throws cold water on our plans.

"What if they search us?"

Although it irritates us to hear his opinions, this one makes sense.

Jack again stands up and commands attention. "He has a good thought there. I think they will search us before we leave the courtyard to come home at night. We have to think of some place to hide the food and get it later when we are working on the other buildings cleaning up the broken boards and tiles. It will take us two days to haul that stuff from the trucks and after that when they search us and find nothing they won't suspect a thing when we are working on cleaning up the outside area."

Jack shuffles his feet before continuing, "As to finding a place to hide the food and getting it there, well, that's going to be a big problem." Jack is through speaking and slowly joins the rest of us sitting on the floor.

The leader declares, "All in favor of this plan signify by saying 'Aye.'"

Every man responds with an approving, "Aye."

"Now then," he begins, "Who has some idea as to where to hide the food?"

I can picture in my mind the area where we have been working all day and try to remember a place that could be easily reached in our normal routine without drawing attention from the guards. Suddenly the answer dawns on me and it is my turn to speak.

"The idea I have in mind is a bit complicated and yet quite simple."

Putting my hands in my back pockets, I go on, "When we were waiting for the guards to eat their dinner today, we were right next to a pile of junk the Germans must have pulled out of the fire the day before. I noticed an old beat-up trunk partially covered by other boxes. If you remember, after the guards finished eating, they sat around talking and never paid any attention to us. Now, if we had the food in our possession at that time we could slip it into that trunk and leave it there for a few days until

120

we are through unloading the trucks. Then when we start cleaning up the yard area, we could take it out. Of course, that means the food will have to be taken tomorrow morning, stored at noon time and then no more taken during the rest of the day. If about five men hide the food in their pockets just before dinner, it won't be noticed throughout the morning and also by that time the guards will have relaxed their watch a little. These five men will sit near the trunk and wait for the proper moment to put the food in it. Meanwhile, the rest of us must overcome our curiosity in trying to see if the five men are doing their job right and concentrate on covering up for them. We wouldn't want to create any movements that will attract the guards' attention to us. We must make sure if they do glance in our direction that they cannot see that food is being hidden. I don't think the pile of junk is any good to anyone so it won't be hauled away until the whole area is cleaned up and then taken away with the rest of the scrap." Now feeling as Jack did after his long speech, I nod my head and slide to a sitting position on the floor.

"Now we're getting some place," remarks a man in the front of the room.

"It's beginning to take shape," the six foot leader answers. "Of course, there are still alot of dangers that have not been taken into consideration. First, if just one of us tries to take some food and hide it on himself without being one of the five men and he attempts to bring it back here for his own private feast, it could ruin the whole plan. If he is searched and caught, it will affect all of us and we may not go to work on the trucks the next day. Also, it may cut out our nightly ration of bread and so nothing could be gained by this."

The men are listening closely.

He continues. "Second, if any of the five men in their eagerness to do the job right, should take a chance and try to hide some food when the situation does not call for it, it could also be disastrous."

He shifts his body, putting his weight on his other foot and sums up the plan in detail to make sure we have it straight.

"Now then, we come to the real problem," he ventures as his eyes glance over the entire group. "I need five men who are willing to take the risk of carrying the food to the truck." He smiles. "Any volunteers?"

Jack and I stand in unison with eight other men. One of them is the man with the timid voice. He evidently realizes he has shown a lack of courage in his earlier statements and now he wants to show the men he will do his part. His name is shouted down for fear his nervous actions might arouse the guards. That leaves nine of us. The leader strokes his beard in thought.

Jack whispers, "It will be hard to choose any of these men when actually none of us knows the other's qualifications."

"There isn't any way for us to take a vote on who will take part in this. Is it alright if I pick the five men?" the leader suggests.

Voices of approval show the respect the group has for him and the way he is handling the meeting thus far. He has been impartial and listened to every man's suggestions; even the timid man's.

The leader looks over the nine men standing before him. He doesn't want to hurt any of our feelings. His eyes dart back and forth as he tries to make up his mind. The room is quiet and only the wind as it howls around the corner of the building, breaks the silence. He lowers his gaze and with one hand on his chin, paces up and down in front of us, trying to come up with a solution.

Suddenly he stops.

Speaking to the nine of us, he sets forth, "Do any of you want to sit down and let the others take part in this, now that you know we have enough men for the job? We all know you are willing to do your part but it would make it much easier for me if I didn't have to choose between you."

Three men look around and shrugging their shoulders, sit down. That leaves six of us still standing. The leader has a problem.

Jack is speaking, "Why not let six of us do it? I'm sure one extra isn't going to foul up the job."

"I don't see where it would hurt to let six men do it either. In fact, it might make it that much easier because each man would not have to carry so much. It wouldn't be as noticeable to the guards," the relieved leader states. "I would suggest that you six men get together and make your own plans for hiding the food in the trunk. And also, as to how you are going to hide it on your person when you take it from the trucks."

The meeting is ended and conversations start up in little groups scattered around the room.

The six of us thread our way to one corner to work out our plans. Jack takes over the group with a suggestion of first finding out ways and means of hiding the cans and packages under our clothing.

It is agreed, no bulky articles will be taken for fear they willbe seen by the guards' searching eyes. The fact is also pointed out by one of the men that the small cans and packages probably contain dehydrated food and will go farther in feeding the group when the time comes.

I suggest that if we tuck our pants cuffs in our shoe tops, it will be a good hiding place for small things that will not stick out too much. Also our shirt pockets will be alright because with our field jackets over them, the bulges will not show. We can also stick a few items inside our shirt and keep them at our hips because our arms will cover them as we walk.

Our pants pockets and helmet liners are voted down as the bulges will show in the pants and the helmet liners might accidentally be knocked off and give away our plan.

Also we agree not to try and carry too much as one false move with a big load would give the guards a tip off as to what is going on.

My idea of the pants legs is improved upon by Jack as he shows us with his wallet that the corners of the wallet are noticeable under the pants as it settles around the shoe top. But when he sticks his wallet in his sagging long underwear leg, and it is held close to the leg, the pants blouse out in their natural shape. He also states that we can carry alot more that way. He is right.

With that problem settled, we start discussing the time and the way we will slip the articles into their hiding places.

It is our plan to have the other men hand us the cans while a disturbance is being created. We will be a few steps away from the truck and some men will block the view of the guards at the proper moment. It won't be necessary to pay attention to the guards outside, as we can go with a group of other men around us, one at a time and not be noticed.

Since I know the location of the trunk in the pile of junk, I am chosen as the one who will open it and conceal the loot inside. The others will pass the food to me as we sit in a group at dinner time. The plan sounds good to us and we are jubilant with thoughts of food that will soon be in our possession.

Later, as Jack and I are trying to sleep, I begin to see loopholes in the plan and shivers run up and down my spine. "What if something goes wrong? Maybe someone's shirt will slip out from under his belt and a pile of cans will fall to the ground in front of a guard! Or what if one of us is careless in secreting the articles in our pants and a guard sees us? Maybe some of the other men who will be covering for us, will get too curious and keep looking at us? That would surely give us away!"

Jack brings me out of my deep concentration by asking quietly, "What are you thinking about?"

"Probably the same thing you are," I answer.

"Yeah, it looked good when we were suggesting it, but now I wonder if it will work?" he muses.

"It's got to work, Jack! If it doesn't, we sure won't get another chance to try it over again. No dry runs for this operation. The first time will be the real thing."

I try to rest with my hands behind my head, staring at a ceiling I cannot see through the darkness. My feet are beginning to bother me again and I cannot figure out why the circulation from my pounding heart isn't reaching them. I can't keep them still as they itch under the warm field jacket.

Some of the men are sleeping already. Their snores and wheezes give the room an atmosphere of a logging camp after the lights are out. The stench of dirty bodies and sweat soaked underwear fills our nostrils and smarts our eyes. Stockings are packed around the stove and the smell to those near it, is almost unbearable. But when men are tired and sleep means gathering strength for the next day, nothing can stop them from falling into a deep slumber.

Dreams of home and loved ones enter our minds and take us out of this room into a distant land where clean

124

sheets and a soft bed after a shower are common things taken for granted.

I think of the first time I met Jean. It was at the tennis courts when we were just kids. It seems like a century ago and yet it is still fresh in my mind. I have to shake the dream from my head for fear it will put me in a state of loneliness and keep me from getting the sleep I so desperately need for tomorrow's ordeal. Movement is coming from Jack's side of the blanket. I turn and ask what he is doing.

"Just brushing my teeth," he whispers.

Chapter Nine

The room is heavy with the odor of drying socks. Only the snores of sleeping men disturb my vision of being caught while stealing from the Red Cross Parcels. The cigarette of last night still lingers in my irritated throat. It has been so long since my last smoke, I discovered I could not inhale without tears coming to my eyes. If only I had a cigarette now to quiet my nerves.

I am awake when The Brute opens the door to voice his "cheery" good morning. He must hate us. His voice seems more strained these past days as if he is trying to muster all of the cruelty he possesses and put it forth in his words to us.

The rest of the men slowly move from their sleeping positions. When they realize this is the day of the "Big Steal," their actions speed up with anxiety of the coming day's events. The hum of voices fills the room and overflows into the stairway where the guards are waiting.

The door opens and Popeye, his eye having a hard time focusing on us, makes it known that enough times has elapsed for us to get to work.

Not wanting to provoke them with any mistakes on this big day, we hurry out of the doorway and down the stairs. After a wait at the water faucet, we quickly form ranks and proceed to the courtyard. I know it is a sin to steal and yet I am able to condone it in my own mind.

As we enter the courtyard the guards stop us and call for the interpreter. He walks to the head of the group where The Brute is waiting and listens while the wildly gesticulating guard explains to him what we hope will happen. All of us could say in unison what the interpreter is saying, "... and remember men, if anyone attempts to steal any articles from the parcels, they will be shot."

The expectation of working with food and not taking any, when we are starving, will be a great temptation and the guards are aware of this. They expect us to steal some and so we must be extra careful not to be seen when we do take it. This is going to be a very critical day in our lives. If we are caught we will not have to worry about what we will be eating tomorrow. A new crew of prisoners will have to be brought here to carry on our work. It is a gruesome thought and yet we know it can very well be a reality.

The plan the Germans have in mind seems to fit in with ours. The parcels are to be stored in one of the two room houses across the courtyard. This means a long string of guards will be needed to watch the complete operation of transporting them that far. Some guards will be needed at both ends of the line so the men will not have a chance to give into temptation. Although this is their thought, it also helps us to keep our own men in line.

Jack and I stick together throughout the early morning. The parcels on the trucks seem to be in good condition. With thirty-nine men working together and not trying to disrupt the harmony of the operation, we soon empty the few trucks that hold the undamaged parcels. Now we are directed to tackle the burned trucks and the broken packages they hold.

As we have surmised, it takes quite a while to get a load of salvageable goods together to make a load for one man. It gives the rest of us a chance to survey the parcels and see just what they contain.

I feel as though I am in a cafeteria where I can go down the line and choose what I want for my meal. The guards are still watching quite close and it will be difficult to hide anything with them breathing down our necks as we wait. If they give us boxes or bags to carry the loose cans and packages, it would simplify our carrying but complicate our pilfering. One balances the other and yet we do not want any more obstacles in the way.

The timid man drops part of his load and Skinhead berates him for his clumsiness. I notice it draws the attention of the other guards and I file that fact away to be used later.

As the morning progresses, the guards relax their close watch on our handling of the food. We are allowed to bunch up at the side of the truck and when an article is dropped, they do not pay too much attention to it. I can see by the progress we are making that it will take at least two days to clear the charred trucks of their precious cargo. That will give us time to get more food hidden in the trunk.

The morning seems to drag along and I wait until almost

noon time to start on the plan we have devised. I check the points of my clothing that will bear the strain of holding cans in place. My stockings are up on my underwear legs as far as possible to provide a tight bond that will take quite a jolt before releasing.

Going to the area provided exclusively for our daily toilet, I have to strain to show good cause for being there. I want to have a good opportunity to tuck my shirt in all around my belt so it will not slip out under the load it soon will carry. I mention this to the other five men and throughout the course of the remaining time before noon, they also strain for a good cause.

The guards do not bother us. They pay no attention to this innocent act. If they had, they would have seen us meticulously placing our shirts evenly around our waists.

It is getting close to the time for storing the articles in their hiding places. Each of the six of us watch the others to see who will start the ball rolling.

Jack comes to our rescue and we see a can of dehydrated eggs slip into his shirt. In a second another follows and we can see it as it rolls to its nest in the bottom of his underwear leg. When its motion is stopped, it is impossible to detect it beneath the bloused pants leg. The other men at the truck are covering for him as though they are old hands at it.

Soon Jack has five articles stored on his person. He moves forward as it comes time for him to carry his load to the house across the courtyard. Three of the men wait for him to join them and their conversation assures me that any noises the hidden cans might make will not be noticed over their voices.

I am next in line to receive the food to be concealed.

They surprise me! The man in front of me shoves two small cans into my hands. Although I know they are coming, I haven't seen them taken from the pile at the edge of the truck. Quickly I glance about and I know that if a guard is looking at me, he will see by the look on my face that I am guilty of something. My hands fumble with the two cans and I almost drop them.

I have forgotten to unzip my field jacket and I stand petrified. "What should I do?"

Another can, larger than the first two, is shoved

128

against my stomach and I grab for it as the man waits for me to take it. It's as though he is going to do his share in getting the articles to me but will be damned if he is going to be caught with them.

I juggle the three cans in one hand as I reach up with the other to unzip the jacket. I have turned away from the guards' view to do this and in doing so I also have moved out of reach of the man in front of me so that when his arm again comes around to hand me a can, I am not close enough. He reaches farther back to find me and in his panic I can see the can falling from his grasp. I have to stick out my shoe to stop the can's downward motion and I tightly close my eyes as I wait for the noise it will make on the cement floor.

Joker, the man on my right, has seen the catastrophe and comes to my rescue. He quickly stoops and catches the can before it hits the floor. I have been saved.

In a flash I store three cans in my shirt.

Evidently the man in front of me has lost courage in the near disaster and he moves forward past the pile of loose cans. Joker takes his place quickly and soon I have my shirt full. As the next can is handed to me, I intend to put it down my underwear leg but with my shirt full, it won't go past my tight belt!

Again a feeling of nausea overtakes me. I calm myself and find that by holding my shirt out in front and sucking in my stomach, I can force the cans down into my underwear leg. The cold cans make me shiver as they slide into place. I stuff one can into each shirt pocket and know that I am loaded.

By this time the line has thinned out in front of me. I move forward to grab an armful of cans to be hauled to the Krauts' storage room. Completely unnerved, I stroll out into the daylight. Three men are waiting. They surround me as we walk across the courtyard.

My face must be white under my heavy black beard. My legs feel immobile. The cold cans around my ankles make the blood rush inward and in doing so keeps the circulation feeding my weak muscles. They answer my fervent call for action. I walk along with the three men who talk loudly to keep the clanking noises from being heard by the guards that line the path before us. I feel like a pack horse loaded to the hilt with a burden that is to the point of breaking if another can is added.

As I walk stiffly on the well packed snow, men are coming from the opposite direction. I see Jack moving toward me with a slightly different gait than normal. It is undetectable to anyone who is not in on our secret mission. As calm as Jack is and as nervous as I am, I must stand out like a cabbage in a carrot patch. I snap myself out of my zombie state and proceed to the storage room.

Popeye and Chipmunk are sitting on a pile of boxes that we have hauled in earlier. They are supervising the unloading of our arms. Sweat stands out on my forehead as my turn comes to pass in front of them. I bend over to set my load down and in rising my hidden loot clinks and clanks with a deafening sound!

Again the men save me from this dilemma. Joker is behind me and drops part of his load. It fits right in with the noise I am making. Popeye shoves Joker and shouts in German at him for his careless act. I am helpless as the German rifle is raised above his head. Joker quickly bends to retrieve his fallen goods and Popeye evidently loses the lust to strike as he slowly lowers the gun and walks back to his seat.

By this time I am almost outside. I turn to see the two guards laughing at the fright they have instilled in Joker.

The wind outside cools my hot brow and helps me to regain my composure. I slow my pace to let the others catch up with me and cover the noise of the cans with their voices. I keep looking down as I walk to see any obstacles that might make me stumble and let the cans come rolling from their secret place.

As I navigate along I can hear a faintly recognizable sound approaching us. It is one of the other five men laden with hidden food. He hurriedly walks alone as if defying the guards to hear the clanking sounds coming from his swinging legs.

Two of the men with me step in front of him. They stop his forward motion until his three men catch up with him to convey him to the storehouse. They have been walking as fast as possible without attracting the attention of the guards, trying all the time to overtake this fast stepping maniac.

While my three men talk about the cold weather, his men tell him with abusive language to stay with them before he breaks up the whole scheme. He evidently has had the same misfortune as I did; trouble in hiding the food in his clothing. When he left the side of the truck, he did it with speed to get away from the scene as quickly as possible. He realizes this now and the group proceeds down the path.

We near the barn and detect another convoy of food being lugged along by one of the men. Faint tinny noises accompany their voices as they talk about a girl they would like to see when they get out of the service.

The shuffling feet and conversation in the barn covers any noise I might make and I relax for the first time since loading. Somewhere in front of me, are two more men who are either receiving their cans to hide or waiting with a courageous calmness that soon will be dashed to nothing when they start the long trek to the storeroom and find the many things that happen along the way.

I pray to God to make the guards call for their dinner and give me a chance to get rid of my incriminating evidence. The thought gives me another chill. I still have to hide the articles in the trunk without being seen. I wonder if I should attempt to do it? Maybe I should turn it over to one of the other men? No, they are just as nervous as I am. If I do this right, maybe my conscience won't bother me as much over the mistakes I have made already today.

Just ahead something is wrong. Two men have started a scuffle and I know it is to cover one of us six men while he is loading. I hope they do not carry it too far. They push and wrestle around until the crisis seems to pass and then they take their former places in line. The guards' attention has been on them all of the time and they have missed the very action they are supposed to watch for.

Five down and one to go.

I wait while the line in front of me shortens. No disturbances break out so I know the sixth man has made the transaction without any trouble. Now all we have to do is wait for the guards to signal for their noontime break.

Dinner comes just before I reach the head of the line for another load. I am relieved over being freed from the ordeal of passing the inspection team at the other end of the line. I almost shout, "Hooray," but that would give away our secret. Now, if only the guards will eat their dinner in the same place as yesterday, we can sit by the pile of junk that holds the empty trunk.

"Empty trunk!" I gasp, "what if the trunk is full and I have no place to rid the men of the stolen food?" We have planned things so carefully and still we haven't foreseen all the problems that might come up.

I pray the guards will go to the shelter of the wagons as they did yesterday. The weather is cold and a stiff breeze is blowing across the courtyard. The sky is clear and a cold sun is trying to help us by penetrating the cool air and warm it so the guards will be comfortable enough outside eating their food. They could just as easily eat in one of the empty houses that line the side of the high wall.

Before figuring out what I will do with the cans in case we do not sit by the trunk, I survey the situation with a clear head. If they eat in the house, it will be crowded and they won't have enough room to stretch out and enjoy their meal. Also if they attempt to eat in there and leave us outside, it will mean they will have to eat in shifts with some of them outside to guard us. No, they are too greedy for this, so I dismiss this idea from my mind.

"Where else could they eat?" Not in the barns; they are filled with trucks. This leaves only the courtyard and that means they will also use the overturned wagon for a wind break. It eases my mind to know I have solved the problem before getting panicky.

Jack walks by my side and I notice the other four men gathering in the barn doorway. They sidle up to me and I wonder if by some chance the cans are showing through my jacket and shirt. Checking this out by assuming a stance as though I am looking at my shoes, I remember that I alone know where the trunk is and they are to follow me to that spot so the food can be hidden.

I relax again as another crisis ticks off the seconds. We are led to the same place as yesterday for our noon-time break.

The guards settle in front of the wagon as we gain the spot where the trunk lies partially covered by debris. As I look at it, the trunk seems to be covered more than I had remembered. I can see it will be a hard job to get to it and hide the food without being detected.

The Pollack is talking to the other guards and they listen attentively to his slurred speech as he points to us. Some of the guards shake their heads from side to side to signify, "No." The Brute is talking now and he seems to be arguing against whatever the Pollack has said.

If they are contemplating a search, they will be rewarded for their efforts. I have to find out what they are saying so we can get rid of our loads. Calling to the interpreter I ask, "What are they talking about? A search?"

"I can't hear them very well," he comments, "but they are saying something about smoking." He leans forward to catch more of the quarrel going on between the guards.

The Pollack is still arguing his case and The Brute is just as strong against it. For the moment I hope The Brute will win. The Pollack has always seemed as though he is a decent sort of guy but now I am not so sure.

I wonder, "Maybe he has seen one of our men take a package of cigarettes from a parcel and now he wants to search us for it? No, that can't be. The Brute surely wouldn't be against catching us in some incriminating act."

The interpreter calls out, "I think he wants to give us each a cigarette for our good work this morning but, of course, The Brute is against it."

Exclamations of joy spread through the group and The Brute throws up his hands as if to say he will not have any part of it.

The two Polish guards go to the store house and return with two packages of Lucky Strikes for us. As they hand them to the two front prisoners, they are thanked sincerely for their kind thoughts.

The guards return to their meals as I move over to the trunk. The general commotion and noise created by the men passing out the cigarettes gives me an opportunity

to work on the lock of the old trunk. Taking a small piece
of steel from the pile of junk, I force the lock with a
quick motion. The squeak it makes when opening is muffled
by the men's exclamations of enthusiasm over the treat
they are getting.

I pull up my underwear legs, letting the cans roll
free. Gathering them in front of me, I drop them one by
one in the trunk as fast as I can while the guards view
is blocked by the standing men. Whether they are still
standing on purpose or not, they are doing a grand job
of covering the scene behind them.

Next my shirt is pulled from its tightly tucked place
under my belt. A stream of odd sized cans pour forth and
they quickly are placed in the trunk.

As I straighten around to a forward position, I find
the other five men have also been busy. A small mountain
of stolen food lies at my feet.

I fumble at the pile, trying to grab two cans at one
time but I am frustrated in the effort by their resistance
to my shaking hands. Jack can see my problem and rushes
to the rescue. The men are still milling around as we
scoop the cans as fast as possible into the trunk. They
bang together but the men are making enough noise to conceal
it. I drop the last can into the opening and shut the lid
quickly.

"Whew!" I blow.

Jack looks at me and smiles. "You handled it like
a veteran but you sure looked foolish with that pile of
food in front of you."

He laughs quietly and pushes my shoulder in fun.
As he does this, I lose my balance and roll on my back.
I have to laugh also at the way he makes a joke out of
such a serious situation. I roll over on my stomach to
get up and the laugh sticks in my throat. Two weights are
pressing against my chest!

I have forgotten the cans in my shirt pockets!

"My God, what else can go wrong?"

The men toward the front are starting to sit down
as if they know their work of hiding us is finished. My
hands clutch the two cans through my shirt and I must look
like a woman covering her naked breasts.

I whisper to Jack in a pinched tone, "I still have
134

two cans in my shirt pockets!"

The smile leaves his face as he can see the predicament I am in. The men are almost seated.

The guards are watching to see that we thoroughly enjoy the smoke they have given us. No conversation is coming from them as they sit calmly eating their soup. There is no chance for me to raise the lid on the trunk with them watching so closely.

I turn to Jack with a questioning look on my face. Before I can say a word, he has read my thoughts and says, "Don't worry, we'll find a way out of this."

He hands me a cigarette and volunteers a light from his.

As the light has traveled from the front of the group, the men sit down, leaving us exposed to the guards' view.

"Don't try to put them in the trunk or you will be caught sure as hell," he mutters from the corner of his mouth.

Everything has worked fine in putting the other cans away and I know I can't bungle the job with a futile try to rid myself of these last two. As I take a deep puff on the cigarette it bites into my throat. I cough. It will draw attention to me!

My imagination is working overtime and everything I do seems to signal the guards and tell them that here sits a fool who has two stolen food containers in his shirt pockets. Finally I realize that other men are coughing also as they are attempting to enjoy their cigarette.

The picture of being searched and caught drowns my mind and prevents me from trying to come up with a solution to my predicament.

Jack observes, "If you have to, hang on to them until we start working this afternoon and then slip them out and carry them with the rest to the storehouse."

It is such a simple solution and I wonder why I hadn't thought of it? Now all I have to do is hope I am not caught before I can get rid of them.

While the men enjoy their smoke, mine turns my stomach as I worry about the cans.

I lay back on the snow covered ground like the rest of the men so I won't be conspicuous. I am not going to take any chances on drawing the guards' attention to me even in an innocent way.

"How can I be so forgetful? My main purpose for being on earth this day is to hide a supply of food for the other men and I have failed in so many ways. If only I hadn't asked to be one of the six men. I should have sat down when there were too many volunteers." These thoughts scream through my brain and for the first time I wait for our rest period to end.

As I stare at the few white clouds that sail across the cold blue sky, I wish I were up there riding away on one of them. The last one even looks like a ship with an overgrown sail. It rides the wind smoothly and a small piece breaks loose as if it were a ladder coming down for me to ascend on.

Jack notices the cigarette burning closer to my finger tips and does not say anything. Then the cigarette burns my skin and jolts me from my wild day dreaming.

"Looks like your hand got a hot foot," he laughs.

"No kidding!" I answer with disgust.

The cigarette has burned almost to the throw away stage. I realize that if I am to get any enjoyment out of it, I had better hurry.

As I puff, it sears my throat. "Enjoyment - Huh!" But it is a treat and I keep on puffing until I hold one corner of the end in my fingers and puff on the other corner.

"This is a good way to get a blistered lip," I declare.

On the next puff the tobacco gives out and the paper burns both my fingers and my lips as I try to get all of the last smoke into my mouth. I throw the ash into the snow where it spits and sizzles out. My lip is hot and sore. Jack laughs at my plight. I notice his cigarette is gone. He evidently had presence of mind to throw his away before he got burned.

The Brute signals the end of their noon hour and wiping his greasy chin on his coat sleeve, shoulders his rifle and moves toward us. At last the time has come for me to get rid of my two cans.

I loathe giving them back to the Germans after all the trouble I have gone through to conceal them, yet I know it is the only solution. Jack and I alone are aware of the explosive situation.

A calm group of men plod toward the barns to resume our salvage job. The cans seem to be burning my chest as I feel their weight. We are stopped short of the barn doors and the interpreter is called forward. The Brute again explains that anyone caught with stolen goods will be shot.

Jack sends a quick glance in my direction. The interpreter repeats the rules and when he finishes, the men break into grunts of disgust and laughter. My mind screams for them to shut up before they taunt the guards into searching us. As I realize that is exactly what they want to do because they know all the food has been hidden at noontime, I feel a surge of anger come over me.

"What fools you are!"

I can see the terrified look on Jack's face as the guards step closer. They ARE going to search us!

Jack flings his jacket open as if inviting a search and he throws out his chest to show he has nothing to hide. Other men follow suit as I stand rooted to the ground with fright. I am shocked by Jack's action and cannot understand why he invites a search when he knows what it will mean to me.

I ask God to perform a miracle and save me. As if in answer, the guards stop after the first few men and realize that since the men have provoked them into a search they could not possibly be hiding anything. They push us forward into the barn amid laughs and playful slaps on the back by prisoners.

My legs will not move and only because I am in the center of the group for protection am I propelled along with the rest into the barn.

The relief is almost too great for me and I have to fight dizziness to keep my balance. Jack is right there shaking my arm to snap me out of it. We cut into the center of the line at the side of the truck. I turn to thank him and he deftly picks the cans out of my pockets and slides them along the truck-bed into the pile before any of the guards take their positions. If only they knew all the things that have gone on under their noses today they would lose faith in themselves as guards.

I feel as though a tight steel band has been removed from my chest and the smile on my face must tell Jack how

relieved I am. His pat on the back as I face forward in
line seems to bolster my spirits and I know I am safe from
all detection. The near disaster is forgotten as the chill
of the day enters my body and numbs my feet.

The afternoon wears on slowly as the sun settles in
its nest of trees on the horizon. The air cools. With
the brisk breezes whipping around the courtyard, we have
to work fast to keep warm.

The number of trucks yet to be cleared of their charred
packages assures us of at least one more day of labor over
them. That means more food could be stored tomorrow.
It is gratifying to have food put away, even if we still
have many obstacles ahead before actually knowing its
filling goodness in our stomachs.

Popeye calls for the work to come to a halt. As the
last few of us haul a load to the storehouse, the others
are detoured toward the courtyard gate.

When we join the group a thorough search is in progress
and the guards aren't to be denied this time. They start
at our shoe tops and proceed up to our shoulders, down
our sleeves and finish with our helmet liners. The Brute
seems disgusted with us for not having enough guts to try
and sneak at least one article from the parcels.

The rest of the guards act jubilant over the fact
and imagine their authority is being respected.

We laugh inwardly as the last man is being searched
and nothing is found. Every man has kept his word and
we are in good spirits. It has been difficult not to take
food when our hands hold it and our bodies crave it.

Tired and cold but cheerfully warm, we march back
to the schoolhouse and crowd up at the doorway. The door
closes and tired bodies slump to the floor in their own
"stalls." It has been a terrific day both physically and
mentally. Here and there a few smiles break out and when
we finally realize the tension has been lifted, we all
laugh and happily wait for our share of the nightly bread.

Conversations start and heads bob as they recall the
more jovial happenings, especially the search at noon time.
While everyone laughs at their taunting the guards and
the subsequent partial search, I poke Jack and ask, "Shall
I tell them how close we were to being caught?"

His face breaks into the familiar smile while answering, "No, let them enjoy themselves. What they don't know won't hurt them."

I quickly agree with him and in doing so free myself of explaining my forgetfulness.

The Pollack enters with our bread ration and a cheer breaks from the group as they recall his thoughtfulness in appropriating the gift of cigarettes for our noon hour treat.

A smile crosses his face as he sternly motions for silence lest this outbreak place his position with the other guards in jeopardy. He leaves quickly as if to get away from this friendly spirit that is shown toward him.

Jack and I step forward to receive our share and return to our blanket. It isn't until then that I remember we are not going to eat our bread until morning.

The thought of going hungry all night strikes me as foolish. "What if we die during the night? Our bread will be wasted!"

I open my mouth to speak my thoughts and then I see Jack tucking his bread under his shirt. My mouth closes as I realize it is no use trying to talk Jack out of it. I concede in my mind that he is right. It will do us more good in the morning. My bread is gently placed in my shirt as though it is a baby being put to sleep.

I lay back on the blanket and my tingling feet bring me upright again. I have forgotten to take off my shoes. I reach forward and work at the wet laces, being careful not to break them. The shoes stick to my feet as I jerk at them. It's a relief to have them off. My stockings come off with the resistance of peeling an orange. I wiggle my toes and their wrinkled whiteness looks eerie in the darkening room. They are whiter this evening than ever before. The numbness seems to reach up and engulf my ankles. I remember this morning they hurt when I put on my shoes. I wonder why they are numb and I try rubbing them briskly with the blanket. They hurt, yet they are still without feeling. It's a funny sensation.

I lay down and the noise of the other men enjoying their slice of bread comes to my ears. It's torture to save the bread. I clasp my hands behind my head and stare at the dimly lit ceiling. Fifteen minutes pass. Neither Jack nor I speak.

Then turning to face me, he asks, "What 'cha thinkin' about?"

Not answered immediately, he raises up on his elbows and continues, "Hey, Jackson, I asked you a question!"

"Oh, just thinking. You know how it is..."

He rolls over to a better position to get at whatever it is he is fishing for. "Here," he proclaims as he proudly produces half a cigarette, "all the comforts of home."

I laugh then ask, "Where in hell did you get this? Is it part of the one you got at noontime?"

He nods his head with a trace of bashfulness. "Yeah, I didn't want all of it at one time."

I know he is kidding. He has saved it purposely for us to enjoy this evening --- and he wants to talk.

Jack eyes the dark ceiling. He pauses, thinking deeply. "Isn't it funny how many things can happen to a man in a lifetime? Just think, here we are only nineteen years old, all the things we have seen, the things we have done, the things we have been ordered to do, both by the Army and our captors."

Raising himself to a sitting position on our blanket and placing his back against the wall, he continues, "I don't know what the average life expectancy of an American male is but just for the moment, let's say it's about sixty. That means we have experienced less than one third of the secrets our lifetime holds!" He stares into space mulling this over in his mind.

"Holy cow, I don't know if I can go through this two more times!" I joke.

He laughs and pulls out the ever present twig toothbrush, absent-mindedly swishing and twirling it over his white polished teeth.

"It is food for thought, though," I muse. "Wouldn't it be something if we knew what our future life holds for us? If we could look at our own personal calendar and see what we will be doing ten years from today. And maybe even find out the date we'd fall off the Pyramids and break our necks!"

Jack pushes my shoulder. "Knock it off. Don't lose track of what I'm saying."

Using the worn toothbrush for emphasis, he points it at my face and while shaking it, adds, "What if we got back to the States and someone angered us by, say, stealing our girlfriend from us and we killed him. We would be brought to trial on a murder charge."

"Sure would."

"Our defense would be something like this: 'Your Honor,' I'd say while assuming an important looking stance and stern face. 'I consider my deed was provoked because something I held near and dear to me was being taken away and was endangered by an intruder. It was my property and I raised to defend it just as I had done when I entered military life. There I actually invaded the intruder's own private property and killed him wherever and whenever I saw him. He may never have had any idea of taking something personally from me and yet I had to kill him. Then it was an honor and we were praised for it. In fact, if we killed enough men who were our enemies, the war officials would promote us and that meant higher pay. I consider this to be the same act to protect something precious to me. I have killed many men for this reason while in the service.'" Jack turns to me as he finishes and asks, "I wonder what they would do to me?"

"Probably declare you insane and put you away," I remark.

"Come on now," he appeals, "be serious about this."

"Well, they probably would have you plead temporary insanity."

"That wouldn't be right! If it is paralleled to our killing Germans and we are proclaimed temporarily insane, they would give us a Section Eight and put us through the rest cure... or discharge us."

"Well, as far as I'm concerned, they can do what they want with you. I'm tired and I'm going to sleep. When you have it all figured out, let me know so I'll be able to determine whether I'm chumming with a murderer or a hero. Good night." Rolling over with my helmet liner for a pillow, I close my eyes with thoughts of getting a bundle of Red Cross food out of the Krauts' hands and into my stomach. It will be as hazardous as any patrol work and this time the Germans have all the guns.

Jack is still awake and intrudes on my attempt to sleep. "Bob, how do you think we got into this prisoner of war situation?"

141

"It was a set up," I answer.

"Set up? How could the Allies set up losing so many men and so much territory? I mean, we really took a beating. Why, we didn't have enough ammo or food to last two days when they hit us. And as far as stopping them, well, we didn't have a chance. We were far below normal strength as far as men and weapons were concerned. There were gaps between companies --- no communications to rear units and..."

"That's what I mean," I interrupt, wide awake again. "I wonder how many others in this room can tell the same story. I mean, men from different outfits. I'll bet at least ninety per cent were left in the same situation as we were; left wide open to entice the Germans to put on their big push. There we were gaining ground as fast as our supplies could keep up with us and suddenly we were stopped and told to just hold the ground we had. Not only that but we were kept at least two miles from their front lines. Then WHAM! Geez, what a mauling we took. It was a massacre. Only eighteen of us left out of my whole company. No ammunition or supplies to hold out any longer so we had to surrender."

Remembering how we were left out in the open with nothing to fight with, gorges my brain with anger. Looking over at Jack, I clench my fist and smack it in my other palm. "Can you imagine the inhuman orders of leaving us out there like a weak decoy to attract the enemy into swarming over us for the kill?"

Jack looks at me with fire in his eyes, "It all seems clear now. I couldn't imagine how the whole Allied force in our sector got caught short. Do you think it was planned to actually have us wiped out as a means to an end? Why those dirty sons-of-bitches. They always said men were expendable and I guess this proves it. They could spare the men but not the material. That must be why they didn't give us the supplies we needed and the tons of ammo that usually follow right behind us. They certainly had time to get them up to us. I suppose they were afraid that by some miracle we might stop the Germans and ruin the whole operation."

"Yeah," I inject, "and not only that but I think it worked because today I heard alot of rumbling in the

142

distance and it sounded like artillery to me. You see, the way I've got it figured is this; we now must have marched at least a hundred miles back into Germany and the Krauts must have pushed into our lines almost a hundred miles, according to some of the stories the other prisoners have told me. If that is the case, then why do I hear artillery only about twenty or thirty miles from here if the front lines haven't moved back into Germany again? Right?"

Now I'm really getting into it.

"And another thing, the German supplies are being hauled in horse and wagon trains instead of trucks. They wouldn't do that if the haul were more than twenty or thirty miles, would they? Of course, this is all speculation on my part about the location of the front lines. But it seems so real that the truth of the matter is: I've been believing it for some time."

"How soon do you think the war will be over?" Jack questions.

"I don't have any more idea than you do. But I suppose when the politicians and war supply manufacturers have enough money and can settle their petty differences over a conference table instead of across our dead bodies."

"You don't really believe that, do you?"

"No, not exactly, but by the looks of conditions back here; no gas, no signs of military equipment, no nothing, except tired scared Germans, it should have ended a couple months ago. I can't remember when last I saw a German plane and yet our planes are passing over here everyday. It just doesn't make sense, does it?"

"It sure doesn't, but I guess it takes time to mop up the areas we have taken."

Jack scootches forward on the seat of his pants and lies down beside me. He is deep in serious thought again.

The room is dark. I pull my field jacket over my tingling feet and ease them to a more comfortable position. They have started to hurt again and I don't seem to be able to find a way to stop the ache. It's painful to walk over the uneven ground on which we have been working and the muscles in the upper part of my legs feel as if they are one big, big Charley horse. Every movement is torture to me yet I must accept it. When I stop working or when

143

my mind is not deeply occupied in conversation then they bother me the most.

I wonder if I will be able to stand it much longer. I guess I have no choice. The other men are in the same condition and they also have to keep going. If only nothing else happens to me, like those men who were beaten in the woods. They are being made to work regardless of their condition.

Turning to me, Jack breathes, "By the way, have you thought of escape lately?"

"Yes, but with all the things going on these past few days it has been hard to concentrate on it. Why? Have you got any new ideas?"

"No, not exactly, but by going over our conversation I think now would be the time to do it."

"What do you mean?" I whisper.

"Well, if our lines are only twenty miles away, according to your deductions because of the artillery we hear, then that means they may have to move us out of here pretty soon so we won't be liberated. They could move us further back into Germany again. And the odds are that it will be easier to escape now and move twenty miles than escape later and have to travel a hundred miles or more to our lines."

"That's true. But how are we going to get out of such a small bunch without being noticed?"

"I don't know but what do you say we start planning some of the small details now so they will be out of the way when the opportunity comes?"

"That's O.K. with me. Just what do you have in mind?"

"If we could get away from here and move close to the front lines; hole up in a bombed cellar or any hole in the ground that wouldn't be too likely to be searched; then when our Army pushes the Germans back, we would wait until our men pass over us before we come out. Then we'd be safe."

"Yeah, but we may have to stay holed up in one spot without moving for weeks. Where would we get food so we will still be alive to enjoy this freedom? Mind you now, I'm not criticizing your idea because I really think it's good but we have to be realistic about this."

"The only suggestion I have," he states, "is that

144

we cut our bread ration in half each day and save it."

"Me and my big mouth." I concede. "First you talk me into saving it for breakfast and now you are trying to talk me into saving half of it for future use."

I can see it is the only solution but I don't have to like it.

"We could probably pick up some food on the way but that would mean stealing it from the Germans and detection would get us shot."

"Where will we keep this hoard of bread while we're working? They'll be searching us pretty regularly now that we're working on the Red Cross Parcels."

"I was contemplating that while you were thinking of ways to talk me out of it," Jack chuckles.

It's a good thing it's dark so he can't clearly see my jaw drop and my eyes bulge. He does read my mind but I guess it's pretty obvious by the way I have acted.

"Say," he blurts, "how about in the window ledge behind the loosened boards?"

"And have other men steal it from us? Nothing doing. We might just as well leave it out in the middle of the floor as far as I'm concerned."

"How about seeing if we can loosen the trim board below the window and see if we can make a storage space there?"

Without waiting for an answer, he sits up by the window and starts pulling at the board. It comes off quite easily and something falls to the floor.

"What was that?"

"It's a book!" I answer as I retrieve it from the floor. "What's it doing in a place like this? It must be something important to be hidden."

It's too dark and I'm not able to tell what kind of book it is. The covers are hardbound and it seems to be in good condition.

"Let's take off the window boards and see if the moon will give us enough light to see what kind of a book it is," Jack suggests.

"Good idea."

The boards come off quickly. By holding the book close to the window we can make out the letters and pictures but cannot read the German words.

145

Jack flips the pages and reports slowly, "It looks like a text book. You know, a school book. Maybe some German kid didn't want to do his homework and hid it in here. This was a classroom before we took it over for an apartment house."

"By the type of pictures and maps, I'd say it' s either German History or Geography."

"Here's a big map of Germany at the beginning of this lesson."

Jack turns the page and a series of maps on a double sheet catches our attention. Each section of the country is shown in detail. One map has a penciled circle around a small town named, "Heidweiler."

"That's it!" Jack exclaims.

His excitement fires mine and we soon have the map oriented from knowing where the sun rises every morning. Quickly we find other detailed maps of the surrounding sections and place them on the window ledge like a jigsaw puzzle. It takes shape and according to the scale on the map and by figuring out the location of the artillery sound, we know that Trier is the town catching hell. It is only twenty miles away.

Our new found treasure reveals many things we want to know. It shows all of the roads, even the woodsmen's trails through the forest areas. Detailed information in the form of small trees, miniature airplanes and smoke stacks, give us a complete picture of the location of things that will be invaluable to us on the escape route. It is like a gift from heaven.

We talk and plan and laugh until the wee hours of the morning. It is about 3 A.M. when the other prisoners in the room start to complain about the noise of our raised voices. We keep quiet. Sleep is impossible with thoughts of escape fresh on our minds and the coming day's adventure of securing more food in the trunk.

Suddenly a thought strikes me. The Red Cross Parcels! There is plenty of concentrated food that we could take with us on our escape.

I sit up and grab Jack's shoulder, shaking it vigorously. "Jack! Wake up! Listen to me. We can get all the food we will need for our escape from the supply of Red Cross Parcels!"

146

He slowly rolls over and explains, "I've already discarded that idea because it must be well guarded against theft from the villagers, so go to sleep."

"Why hadn't I though of that?"

Jack rolls back and says, "Of course, if we can escape from this room, we can always check the area and see if there is a way to get some of that food. After all, we took it from under their noses in daylight and we ought to be able to get it at night if it isn't guarded too closely."

Darkness covers the smile that crosses my face. He knows it could ruin our plans if we try to get some of that food.

Chapter Ten

Marching into the courtyard to put in another day's labor on the Red Cross Parcels stirs our bodies to new life.

"God, how I hate to work for the Germans!"

With an aching back, swollen feet and hunger gnawing in my stomach, I march differently than I did in basic training. Keeping in step with arms swinging in unison has been forgotten. All I care about is getting to wherever they are leading us.

Before reaching the courtyard, my worn out shoes are soaked from the ankle deep snow. It will be another miserable day for this P.O.W.

As I walk to the center of the yard, my eyes scan the pile of junk to see if our trunk is still there. Seeing it in the same condition as we left it, answers my question.

"What a situation to be in," I mutter to Jack. "We're so close to food, yet we can't have any. It's all I think about."

"Yeah," he answers. "I wonder how much more we can take before we are liberated? I finally realized we are just living from day to day. We don't have too many bright thoughts for the future."

The Brute is again explaining to the interpreter about stealing and shooting It is an old story and sometimes I wonder if death won't be more preferable to being a prisoner.

But I know I have someone to live for. I can't help but look at the exposed white circle of skin on my finger where Jean's ring has been worn until only a few weeks ago. Tears come to my eyes and the magnitude of my loneliness is greater than I have experienced before.

"I love you, Jean, with all my heart and I must live for the day when our dreams can come true. Why must I go through this hell to earn my heaven in your arms?"

Wiping my eyes on my sleeve, I stumble toward the barns where the burned trucks hold our day's work.

The air is cold and the wind whips snow flurries about the courtyard as if a ballet troupe is performing. The freezing temperatures makes the guards huddle in their positions and they are more concerned with keeping warm than watching us too closely. It is easier for us today.

148

Men are working on the truck, bunching cans and handing them to the ones who will carry a load to the storehouse.

As I watch closely I can see a small pile of select canned food slowly being built and nonchalantly being moved toward the edge of the truck. Without knowing the real reason, I would think they were sorting it for the Germans. This is being done in such an open way that I wonder if the men even give a thought to the seriousness of their actions. They are engrossed in their work and the line keeps moving slowly forward as we make our trips and then return to stand in line while the others gather a load.

Popeye and Chipmunk guard the growing pile of salvageable food in the storehouse and they watch to see that we put all our load down. We notice they are smoking Lucky Strikes and are thoroughly enjoying them. The irony of having them smoke "our" cigarettes and eat "our" food is almost too much to bear.

Some of the prisoners reveal their feelings by their grim looks, while others smile, trying to get the butt end for a few puffs for themselves. The two guards enjoy this and make a great show of smoking while having the package of cigarettes in full view. This is a form of cruelty and I vow I will make them pay for it some day.

Shortly before noontime I saunter to the latrine area and again strain to show good cause as to why I am there. While tucking in my shirt tightly around my waist and making sure my socks are well up on my underwear legs, I can hear the "crump-crump-crump" of far off artillery. It amplifies my desire for freedom and all the comforts that come with it. Tonight I'll talk to Jack and really get down to making our escape plans. It has to be soon. Surely they will move us out of this area before long.

"You're next, Bob," Jack verifies as I join the rest of the prisoners at the barn.

Before getting a load in my arms for the Germans, I receive and hide a goodly supply of small canned goods for our own use. I know it is risky and although I am frightened, I am also determined to do my best and not make any mistakes as I did yesterday.

We are stealing the food too early this morning!

I have already made two trips to the storeroom with my hidden loot and still there is no sign of the Germans knocking off for dinner.

Standing next to Jack, I whisper, "I can't figure it out. Those gluttons have never before missed a dinner hour."

Noontime passes and now the six of us are really worried. All the prisoners form small groups and discuss the situation quietly as we continue to work. A tap on the shoulder makes my blood run cold and I slowly turn around expecting to find a guard with his rifle ready to shoot.

It's just the interpreter with an idea.

"I'm going to ask the guards why we haven't had a rest after working all morning," he states.

We all want to find out why our daily routine has been changed.

In a few minutes he returns with the bad news.

"The guards are going to a meeting of their officers this afternoon and so we are to work a short day with no noon break," he reports.

As the terrifying news penetrates my weary brain, an SS trooper appears with two German guards who are strangers to us. They march straight to The Brute, who salutes smartly and receives their few short orders.

Meanwhile, our guards are rounding us up and getting us ready to move out.

It is a horrified group of prisoners who press together with the knowledge that soon we will be searched and six of us will be found loaded. There is no escape and no possible place to get rid of the canned goods.

The Brute is marching toward us while the SS trooper and his personal escort exit through the gate.

The awful silence surrounding our group makes the approaching steps sound like a death dirge. Heavy boots crunch and squeak in the snow. Closer and closer comes our doom until we are ready to riot and make any attempt at escaping the death we know awaits us.

My legs are quivering while sweat trickles down my back. I am rooted to the spot and only a great shock will be able to move me.

Jack stands at my side, his face ashen. Short breaths whistle through his teeth. While every one is in a state of petrified fear, I can easily pick out the six of us with the stolen food.

The Brute is now in front of us and calls to the other guards.

We advance down the path to the gate. When halfway there, they detour us toward the overturned wagon and the pile of trash which hides our trunk. Quietly we sit in our places as the guards take out their dinner plates.

"Wot hoppen?" a voice asks from the center of the group of relieved men.

The interpreter answers, "From what I heard The Brute telling the other guards, the meeting was called off and we are to work our full shift. So naturally the guards have to eat their dinner."

"Naturally," I agree.

Jack affirms, "The ways of God are many." Today it means a reprieve for all of us.

We are seated as yesterday and as the guards eat their late dinner with ravenous appetites, I fill the trunk with another load of stolen food. It is a relief to get rid of it and to know it is safely stored away with no incriminating evidence left on us. I have checked my hiding places three times to make sure I haven't left any on me. I signal the rest to do the same and when they finish I know by their smiles that all is well.

The rest of the day passes without incident and the night finds us in the prison room of our school house.

The main subject of our conversation is the near tragedy of today's events. Laughter breaks out here and there but it is a forced laughter that dies with the chilly thoughts of what might have happened if we had been caught.

Jack turns to me and asks, "What do you think the meeting was all about?"

Rolling over to face him, I answer, "Maybe to discuss the nearness of the artillery and to get orders as to what to do in case it gets closer."

"Wonder why they canceled the meeting?"

"Evidently they had a change of plans. But why? Well, I've been trying to figure that out. Did you notice how close and heavy that artillery was today just before noon?"

"Yes, I did, and maybe that's the answer," he replies. "It was much heavier this morning than any previous time and maybe the big push is on. That means if we are going to escape, it will have to be soon. They will probably move us in a week, if not sooner. It all depends on how fast our boys push them back." The serious look on his face gives added strength to his deductions which seem logical to me.

"What should we do, make a break for it now?" I ask.

"No, not yet. We'll have to make plans and be set for it. No use going off half-cocked and snafu the works."

"Well then, let's make plans for the night after tomorrow and see what we can come up with! We can't wait too long or it will be too late," I retort.

"O.K.," he agrees. "Now, let's get that map and figure where we will go after we leave here."

I reach up and help him remove the trim board that holds our precious map. After taking off the lower boards that block the window, we piece the map together on a dimly lit window ledge and start making plans.

"We could go almost straight cross-country for Trier and travel only at night."

"I figure we won't have to go too far because the way the artillery is pounding, it won't be too long before the Allies push over us and we can come out of our hiding place and be free men."

Jack adds, "We'll want to go at least eight or ten miles the first night so we won't be caught up in the search for us, which we know The Brute will head up after he finds out two of his prisoners are missing."

"If luck is with us, we could make that distance the first night. And with all the activity going on up toward that artillery, the whole German Army must be prowling around there. We will be less apt to be noticed in the confusion than if we try to go through a less active area where any movement would cause attention."

"Yes," Jack informs me, "and if we save our bread for two more days, it will be enough to keep us for a week if it has to. By that time we can make up new plans if the big push isn't coming fast enough to suit us."

"It's settled then," I whisper. "We will make our escape two nights from now."

Jack nods approval and takes a few of the small nails from the window boards and pins the map together, carefully placing it in his pocket. Then he puts his handkerchief over it and wads it up to make it look natural.

I'm thirsty and tell Jack I'm going to ask for permission to get a drink of water.

The Pollack is sitting on the bottom step daydreaming. At my appearance he rises and questions why I have come out of our room. In my G I German I explain I want a drink and he lets me pass without further notice, although he does step outside the doorway and waits in front of the building for me.

I can see fairly well from the cold light the moon gives as I walk around to the back of the building.

Locating the faucet is easy and as I place my rusty can up to it, I bump the wall and knock the can out of my hand. It falls with a splash into the barrel. Reaching down I grope in the barrel up to my armpit to find the can that has settled at the bottom. My hand encounters small cubes in the barrel and I draw some out to examine them. They are diced potatoes!

The elation of finding such a hoard of food is almost too much for my hungry body.

"The guards' soup will be a little thinner tomorrow!"

Stuffing a handful into my mouth and chewing the raw potatoes sends a shiver through my taste buds. The icy chunks melt in my mouth as I gulp my second handful. I run my tongue along my teeth to take the pain out of them as they come in contact with the frigid food. Thinking of Jack upstairs with a hungry stomach, makes me realize I have to get some of these for him.

Dipping my can in the barrel, I come up with water and potatoes. I tip the can and by cupping a hand over the edge, drain the water off. I fill my field jacket pockets with cubes. Then I fill my can with water and start back.

It is getting to be an old story now, sneaking things under the guards' noses but just the same I am scared as I walk past the Pollack and up the stairs with the same slow speed we always use. My legs cry out to run but my brain holds control and I casually gain our doorway. Opening it with a shaking hand, I lean against it to recover my jangled nerves and I close the door.

Quickly I cross over to Jack and burst out with the good news.

He sits up with a bolt and grabs my arms to shake me with joy.

I empty my pockets and place the diced potatoes in the can of water and hang them inside the stove door on a piece of wire. Now we must wait until the potatoes boil for our feast.

In a few minutes I open the door a little to find the water just starting to bubble. I look over to Jack and make a circle with my thumb and first finger, just like the French do when they signal everything is O.K.

It is dark in the room and I don't know if he sees my signal or not but the excitement bubbling inside of me is way ahead of the boiling water.

When I can stand it no longer, I withdraw the can from the stove and find it is too hot to handle. I almost drop it and grab a drying sock from the top of the stove to use as a hot pad. My fingers are burning but I do not dare spill it even if my hand burns to the bone.

I carry the can over to Jack and we wait while it cools. I can see a smile on his face as he anticipates the food. It makes me feel good that for once I have supplied him with something in exchange for all he has done for me.

Since we have no spoons, we dip our fingers in the can and enjoy the lumpy mess as much as of it had been cooked by a master chef in the finest hotel. We will sleep well tonight knowing we have saved our full bread ration and yet have eaten better than all the other men.

The morning comes too fast.

We have emptied the trucks of their food and today is the day we will clean up the courtyard of debris and also try to get the canned food out of the trunk and home to our room. According to our plan, we won't be near any canned goods as far as the guards know, so we do not anticipate a search before going home tonight.

"Today will test the mettle of the men," Jack declares.

"Sure will," I agree.

Every man is to carry out at least one can so if anyone is caught all of us will be involved and maybe they will not shoot the entire crew. It is a big chance but the psychology of it seems logical. Everyone agrees to it, even the timid man with the red hair. He was reluctant at first but with thirty-eight men staring at him, he decided to go along with our plan.

The day is warmer than usual and the snow crunches under our feet as we march out of the schoolyard and down the road.

Jack is behind me and his early morning "burp" makes a smile come to my lips. It is forced by him but he just wants me to know he enjoyed the potato dinner we had last night.

The wind has vanished, leaving behind a few wispy breezes that carry the warm air in front of them. It looks like a glorious day. White fleecy clouds, unusual so early in the morning, dot the sky.

As we reach the farmer's barnyard where the chips are made, our rank is detoured into it and the other rank is marched out to the woods.

It is a jolting surprise! I fully expected us to work in the courtyard to finish cleaning it up. I wonder why they have marched us to the barnyard.

When our crew has the buzz-saw going, I ask Jack, "What do you think of this change in plans?"

Shaking his head he vacillates, "The only thing I can figure out is that they want to get as much wood cut as possible before being pushed back by our Army."

"Yeah, but it sure throws cold water on our plans for the canned food."

"Do you want me to tell them that?" Jack quips. "Maybe they will change their plans for us!"

"Tell them if you want to," I laugh.

Some of the other prisoners are shaken by this change and the idea of going without food puts them on edge. Tempers flare and threaten to create a situation the guards will have to handle in their own cruel way.

The buzz-saw gives us the usual trouble throughout the morning; coughing, misfiring and stopping every few minutes. The irregular running of the motor is loosening it from its mounting and I can see it will break loose before the day is over.

Looking at Jack and pointing to the motor mount, I shake my head. "Don't tell the guards or they will want us to fix it now before something breaks. We want to delay this work as long as possible. Let's just let it go."

155

Jack nods in agreement.

A young German boy, about twelve years old, steps out of the farm house and sidles over to watch us. He doesn't seem afraid of us and soon he is standing alongside me with his skinny hands shoved in his coat pockets. The blonde tousled hair is topped with a bright orange knitted cap that is pulled down over his ears. A long black jacket reaches to his knees and keeps the winter cold away from his frail body. High rubber boots complete his insulation. He is either very sick or else undernourished. A pouting face that never seems to smile, looks questioningly at us whenever we speak.

Another log is pressed against the dull blade and the whining noise covers our voices. I can see the belt coming off and since it takes just as much time to straighten it on the pulley as it does to pick it off the ground, I reach for the lever to shut off the motor. Just as I grab the lever, the belt flies off and jerks the motor sideways, ripping out the rusty bolts and nails that hold it in position.

"Well, that's that," Jack jokes. "Another half hour shot. I suppose we will never reach our quota today and here I was going to ask for a raise."

We all laugh at him until the German boy speaks up in perfect English.

"I'll get some new bolts for you from the barn."

Our mouths drop open and we stare at his retreating back as he strides away.

Then turning to face each other, the five of us stammer at the same time, "Did you hear that English?"

Joker responds, "Where in hell did he learn that? He must have understood every word we said this morning. It's a good thing this saw was acting up so we didn't have time to discuss our hidden food."

We all agree with Joker and in our minds we wonder how close we are to being discovered.

Joker continues, "That food is beginning to be more trouble than it's worth!"

One of the other men adds, "Right now it's worth nothing if they don't let us clean up the courtyard and get it out of the trunk."

The boy is returning with a handful of assorted bolts.

156

As he approaches us, we stare at him as if he is someone really important. He hands Jack the bolts.

"Hey, kid, how come you speak English?" I ask.

His reply makes my words sound as if they have come from an illiterate. He looks at me and clearly explains, "My father is a professor of English in Berlin. I am visiting my uncle while my father is busy. I could see by your perplexed faces that you would not be able to repair the engine if I did not give you some assistance. Is it true all Americans are as ignorant as you?"

My face must be turning purple from the verbal slap and I want to grab him and pound his head against the stacked wood. His insolence is almost too much for me but I keep control of myself and bend down toward him. He backs up a step or two and faintly smiles. I can see that he is trying to provoke me into some rash act where I will end up being punished by the guards.

I look at Jack and he breaks up laughing. Slapping my back, he jokes, "They train them from babies over here."

"Yeah, I guess so," I mutter. "He sure took me by surprise. I guess the best way to handle him is to just ignore him until he leaves."

Turning, I walk toward the motor, saying, "Come on, let's fix this broken down wreck the Krauts call a motor."

The boy is gone when I turn around to see how he has received that remark.

"Evidently he is is disgusted with us foreign cavemen," I point out.

In a way I don't blame him. We surely haven't put too much effort into our work this morning. I survey the bearded, disheveled group of prisoners swarming around the warm motor. We do look like cavemen!

I am glad he has left.

Jack comments, "Our English IS deteriorating as well as our bodies. Let's try to do better."

The wrench and hammer provided by the guards gives us no alternative but to repair the loosened motor.

The "chip-chip-chip" of axes wielded by our fellow prisoners fills the air with a disturbingly monotonous noise.

"Damn, I hate to see that pile of chips growing larger," mutters Joker. "Everyone of them is helping the

German war effort."

I agree. It is a sorry situation to see starving, freezing, tired men, work to help their captors delay the day of liberation. We are actually working against ourselves and all the time we know if we do not work, we will not live to see the liberation. It is a morbid choice.

During the early afternoon the men are grumbling among themselves with regard to the Germans eating a dinner while we have nothing to eat. The topic soon turns to the food we have hidden and the treat it will be to taste something different than stale bread.

The timid man with the red hair is working with the detail on the wagon-sled, hauling chips to the barn. He is strongly voicing his opinion against trying to get the food out of the trunk. As far as he is concerned it isn't worth the risk.

The man he is arguing with tells him, "Shut up before they find out about it!"

He haughtily answers the man, "I don't have to shut up!"

This creates an explosive situation and soon they are standing toe to toe arguing loudly. The one trying to calm the red headed prisoner suddenly reaches down to his shoe and withdraws a homemade knife he fashioned from an old file.

Snarling at the red head, "Shut up and get to work or I'll fix you!" He brandishes it under the man's chin.

The timid man is frightened and makes a move to defend himself.

Thinking he is taking up the fight, the man with the knife lunges and cuts a jagged gash across his face. Blood pours down the bearded cheek and his mouth opens to let forth a terrified scream.

The guards are on top of them by this time, and using their rifles as clubs, beat them senseless.

We stand petrified as we see our chances of more freedom being dashed away with this outburst of temper and the flashing of a weapon.

As the two lie on the ground, The Brute calls to the other guards and gives them orders to bring all of us together.

We are pushed to the center of the barnyard and the

158

interpreter is singled out.

He listens as The Brute explodes his temper on the group. Every few minutes the infuriated guard stops and gives the interpreter a chance to pass on his statements.

I'm not sure they are verbatim but the gist of the tirade is that we are ignorant animals who fight amongst ourselves and this shows good reason why the Germans will eventually win the war.

This outbreak means no rations tonight and if any more disturbances break out we will be shot!

Meanwhile the guards are lining us up single file in front of The Brute. He passes his rifle to Popeye and starts an intensive search of every man's clothing from shoes to helmet liners, looking for weapons.

As he comes down the line, he gives his opinion of each man when he finishes and pushes him aside. Jack and I are far back in line and standing behind him I wonder why he is shaking so. I know him to be a brave man and we have been searched many times before without him acting as he is now. Sweat stands out on his neck and his head is visually shaking.

I tap him on the shoulder and ask, "Jack...?"

Before I can ask him what's the matter, he turns his head slightly and whispers out of the corner of his mouth, "The map, I've got it in my pocket!"

I wish I hadn't asked.

I am as frightened as he is. If they find the map and decide it is espionage information, he will be shot. If they think it is for escape purposes, they will do the same.

The Brute is half way down the line and two more knives are found. He is furious!

The two beaten men are regaining consciousness and moaning in their agony. If they are not shot it will be a miracle.

I wonder how much questioning it will take for the timid red head to divulge the reason for their argument. If he talks, we may all be shot for stealing food!

Tension mounts as each man is searched. If The Brute finds any more weapons I'm sure it will go bad for us.

The straight line we originally formed is sagging now as each man tries to watch the progress of the search.

We are concerned with the outcome as much as the guards. With our Army so close, they are getting very touchy.

As The Brute moves farther down the line, I can see he is tiring of his work. The anger he puts into it is sapping his great strength. Calling for the Pollack to help him, is a relief for Jack. It might mean an easier inspection.

The Pollack moves forward to start his searching and turns in between Jack and me. That means Jack will be The Brute's last man to search!

The situation is worse than before.

As I expect, the Pollack does not search too close and finishes the rest of the line before The Brute reaches Jack. He calls to the Pollack and asks where he started. When the Pollack points down the line, The Brute thinks he is pointing at Jack instead of me.

Jack is saved! The search is over! Jack's only comment is, "Whew!"

We are pushed back to work and proceed quickly to our task. It is a reprieve from being shot and every man works a good deal harder than he has all day.

The two men who started the fight are left on the ground to regain their senses. They remain there until the work day ends. Stiff and sore, they are carried to the school house; lucky men who can thank God for still being alive.

Jack has fully recovered from his fright and smiles as he thinks about the hidden map. Looking at me he shakes his head as if to say, "I'm the luckiest man alive."

Since the men in the woods have been left out of the search this afternoon, they receive their shakedown as we stop in front of the school house. They have no idea what it is for but know something is up when they see two beaten men being carried out of the barnyard to join them on the march home.

When we reach the privacy of our room, Jack withdraws the map from his pocket and stares at it. He looks up at me and contends, "Who would think possession of a small piece of paper like this could bring such a scare to a man?"

With that, he takes the trim board off the window frame and places the map back into its hiding place until it is needed for our escape. He replaces the board and slides down onto the blanket with me.

"Well, no bread tonight means we really should postpone our escape until we have a little food saved up to tide us over. What do you think?"

I agree with him, though I hate to do so. I know we will need food to sustain us if we are to hide for more than two days.

It is tormenting to think of waiting when everything has been working so smoothly. We talk of ways to escape and decide to rip the blanket into strips and use as a rope to lower ourselves out the window when the time comes.

Weary after the day's ordeal, we doze into a light sleep for an hour. The noise of another wagon load of supplies moving toward the front line, wakes us to remind our hungry stomachs that food is needed.

Jack asks, "I wonder if the cook would have any more diced potatoes?"

"I'll go see."

Taking his can and mine, I make my way to the door and ask Chipmunk if I can get a drink of water. He passes me on and follows me outside. I walk around the back of the building and turn on the faucet. The barrel is still beneath it. Groping with my hands, I fill my can to the brim with cubes and hide it under my jacket.

As I walk around the corner of the building, I notice Chipmunk has moved out by the roadside to watch the wagons pass. Hurriedly I return to the barrel and dump the water out of Jack's can onto the snow. Filling the second can to the brim with diced cubes, I quickly stride back to the front of the building. Before entering the doorway, I cough lightly to let Chipmunk know I am back and going up the stairs. He turns and seeing me enter the doorway, goes back to watching the wagons as they creak along the slippery road.

As I reach Jack's side, I draw the two cans from under my jacket and hold them out to him.

"Ummm," he says. "Beets."

"What?" I exclaim as I pull the cans back to see what they contain. There they are, bright red beets. "Oh, nooooooo," I groan. "I can't stand beets." The letdown is terrific after visualizing a full can of potatoes for each of us.

"What's the matter?" Jack questions. "Beets are good for you. Put a little color in your checks."

I can hardly speak. "I've never liked beets for as long as I can remember but... I'll try to get to like them tonight."

Jack takes the cans and hangs them in the stove, while I dejectedly flop down to the floor. Talking to myself, I try to convince my taste buds that beets will be good for me. It doesn't work.

After only two bites I almost vomit. I hand my can to Jack. The noise he makes sucking his fingers makes my stomach turn and I get up and remove a few window boards to look outside and try to get my mind off the beets.

The wagons are still passing; their loads shifting as they jounce along the rough road.

The pounding of far off artillery breaks through the night and makes the scene seem like a wagon train of pioneers crossing the plains as a thunder storm threatens to bog them down.

Shouts of loud conversations accompany the wagons as they pass up the street and out of sight.

"I hope our planes catch them in the morning and blast them to hell." With that thought in my mind, I board up the window and lie down.

In the morning as I am awakened by the shouting of guards at the door, I automatically move to get going.

I have forgotten to take off my shoes last night and my feet are sore and stiff. It pains me to step on them and I almost fall trying to walk down the stairs.

Today we march past the farmer's barnyard and head toward the courtyard, the burned trucks and the trunk where our food is stashed.

There is an anxious moment until I spot the trunk. It is setting there with the other debris, out in the open just like Poe's "The Purloined Letter."

Separated into small details, we are scattered around the courtyard to finish clearing up the area. Very little conversation comes from the men as we think about the chance we will be taking when we carry the stolen food home tonight.

The huge barn timbers resist our efforts and only

by joining with other groups are we able to separate them from the fallen buildings. Scrap lumber and most everything that looks as though it can be used again, is placed in neat piles around the yard. By noon the area is beginning to look orderly and the guards call a halt while they sit by the overturned wagons and eat.

While they eat, we quickly remove the food from the trunk and slide the cans forward to the men until it is all passed out. We each have at least two cans and the assortment is evenly distributed.

As I am groping in the bottom of the trunk to get the last cans, I discover an old German harmonica. This is really a prize and I reverently place it in my shirt pocket. It looks in good condition so I'll try to blow a few songs on it tonight. Although it has been a year since I last played, I feel as though any kind of entertainment will boost our morale.

Jack has seen me take it out of the trunk and asks, "Can you play it?"

I mysteriously answer, "That remains to be heard."

The afternoon passes quickly and as the dying rays of sunlight peek over the courtyard wall, we are assembled by the front gate and marched without further ado to the schoolhouse. No incident mars the quiet tension of the group and gaining the inside of our room is a relief.

We have made it!

Our tall leader quickly passes word to the overjoyed group that we must not show our loot until later tonight after we have our bread rations from the guards.

Every man agrees. Their faces show the happy spirit that has been awakened in them.

Jack and I survey the group with a smile. It is almost vulgar to see a group of human beings so ecstatically happy over having one of the basic elements of life, food. There are rich men, poor men, executives and blue collar workers, all thrown together for a time with exactly the same treatment and opportunities and now we are all the same. The primitive acquisition of food for our very lives is the factor that bonds all of us together.

I am brought back to reality by the opening of the door as Popeye enters with our bread ration. He stays until it is evenly distributed, then casting a crosseyed glance over the group so happily enjoying their meager fare, leaves us alone with our thoughts.

Jack and I are saving our bread to help with our escape plans. Watching the others eat signals my stomach and starving body to begin an internal gnawing. I have to find something to take my mind off the food.

Remembering the harmonica in my pocket, I fish it out and proceed to take it apart and clean it. I find it is in surprisingly good condition and with Jack's assistance we soon have it back together.

Placing it to my lips and blowing softly, a beautiful tremelo of music sounds forth. It is a wonderful sound; a thing of beauty and deep tenderness. The noisy, buzzing undertones of the men stop the instant they hear the notes.

All faces turn toward me as I start to play, "Home Sweet Home."

It is the first song I learned to play when I was a boy. The easy manipulation of the tongue and hands in coordination makes the song pour out with all the sentiment for which it was composed.

As I finish and look up, the silence is a vacuum. I can see a faraway look in every man's eyes along with a few tears. For an instant the men are motionless and then they all begin to whisper and come toward me. It's as if they have never seen this small instrument before.

Jack breaks the silence with the casual words, "If you will give him some air, maybe he will play another tune."

I haven't given much thought to my repertoire and am now in a quandary as to what songs I actually know. One of the old time Polish polkas comes to mind and after quickly mulling it over, I stomp my foot and begin to play.

The room fills with laughter and the thud of stomping feet. The men choose partners and gaily hurl themselves around the room, dancing with complete abandon, their huge G I shoes flying through the air.

Within a minute the door opens and the guards enter with rifles at a ready position. They expect to find a riot but as they look over the situation, smiles break out on their faces.

All but one Polish guard and Eightball turn and leave. These two close the door and stand for an hour watching the weak prisoners show more life than they have seen for two months. They clap their hands with the non-dancers in time to the music. Some of the men tie handkerchiefs around their heads and field jackets about their waists, becoming the "belles of the ball." A stag line forms to cut in on them.

I turn from polkas to the old favorites; barbershop singing by raspy voices fills the room with human warmth. We are enjoying ourselves for the first time in months and a pent-up party spirit prevails.

When Eightball and the Pollack leave, Joker cries out, "Let's eat!"

The room floods with laughter and cans of food appear out of their hiding places. We open them and enjoy the meat, cheese and dehydrated eggs from the food parcels.

The problem of disposing of the cans is solved as I play another polka. Half the men dance and stomp their shoes on the cans right in time with the music. When they are all flattened they make a surprisingly small pile and are quickly deposited behind loose boards in the walls.

With full stomachs and weary bodies, we call it a night and lie down to sleep.

But before Jack and I can sleep, our thoughts turn to planning our escape. We talk of it again and decide that tomorrow night will be the night. The endless wondering of when we will try it now turns into the anxiety of getting away without being caught.

We sleep deeply, lulled by the agonized creaking of wheels on the nightly wagon train plodding toward the front lines with its meager supplies.

In the morning as we march to the woods to work, a huge flight of American bombers roars overhead. They must be going straight to some strategic target that as yet is still secured by the Germans. Their escort fighter planes zoom around them as bees watching over a hoard of honey. It is a beautiful sight to see as their silvery wings flicker in the dawn's first light. We can see the guards are fascinated by the open audacity of the bombers coming over to make another daylight raid.

Jack comments, "There will be many more raids before this war is ended. I think the Krauts are going to learn pretty fast that they are not a superior race."

165

During the afternoon our entire work group develops mass diarrhea, the end result from the rich food of last night.

The guards can't understand what is happening to us. It is weakening and soon the logs we are carrying are too much for our waning strength. As I carry one down the hill with wobbly legs, my feet slip out from under me with such speed that I am unable to throw the log from my shoulder as I fall.

The log twists my back and lightening-like pains course through my entire body.

The Brute is standing nearby and since the day's work is already progressing slowly, he is provoked by the thought that one man might be completely out of commission. Striding over to me, he grasps my arm and lifts me bodily from the ground. Bringing himself around behind me, he pushes my arm up into a murderous hammerlock and pounds on my elbow with the butt of his hand.

The pain is fierce and only the shock of the fall keeps me from passing out completely.

As he lets go, I fall flat on my face in the snow and slowly try to gather my strength. I struggle to a kneeling position and brace myself with one hand on a tree. As I hold this position, shaking my head to clear it of pain, his heavy boot thuds into the middle of my back and knocks me out completely.

The cold snow on my face revives me somewhat and I roll over very slowly. My arm and back have vicious pains jabbing through them. Legs that seem half paralyzed, move and ever so slowly I gain a standing position with the aid of the small tree by my side.

Bright lights and dancing black spots fill my eyes. Resting for a few minutes clears my head and I notice the long line of weary, stumbling men plodding down the hill. Their loads are too heavy for their frail bodies.

Anger wells up in me but will not get me anywhere. I have to replace this surge of indignation with thoughts of revenge.

Stumbling along, using trees as hand holds, I reach the foot of the hill where the wagons are being loaded with logs. I know I am in no condition to carry a log and I hope they may permit me to help load logs instead.

I join the loading detail and try to do my share. There is no strength in my back or arm and although my efforts are futile, no one interferes with me.

The afternoon is agonizingly long but it finally ends as I pray for strength to keep on my feet.

The long walk back to the schoolhouse is a frantic race for my mind to control my movements. As we enter our room, Jack helps me to our blanket and I lie down to rest. The first thing I think of is our plan to escape tonight but Jack will have nothing to do with it.

"Listen," he admonishes, "we wouldn't have a chance with you so weak you can't walk. Why, with that arm twisted the way it is, you wouldn't be able to hang onto the blanket to let yourself out the window! No, we can wait until tomorrow night."

I know he is right but I hate to admit it.

Again we save our bread and go to sleep.

Despite the pain, I force myself into the morning's routine: work until noon, watch the guards eat, work until daylight fails and plod back to the schoolhouse. The only difference today is the increasingly loud and steady pounding of the artillery in the near distance.

Four flights of bombers pass over during the day and we know that military activity in the area is growing by leaps and bounds.

Back in the room, Jack asks me how I feel.

Except for being quite stiff, I feel in good enough condition to try our escape and I tell Jack so.

It is a cold night. February's last days are kicking up a good storm. The wind howls around the corner of the building and snow is falling thick and heavy.

"This is good weather for us," I whisper. "The guards will not be alert to challenge our movement and the snow will fill our tracks, leaving little possibility of being trailed and caught."

Jack pockets the map and starts tearing the blanket into strips, knotting it into a strong rope.

As midnight approaches we have our bread supply stuffed inside our shirts and we are ready to go. Quietly I remove the boards from the window and look outside for signs of life. Evidently the heavy snowfall is blocking the supply train and the scene outside is void of any movement.

167

Opening the French type windows is a chore of controlled persistence. They squeak and groan on their rusty hinges.

Knotting the blanket-rope around two of the window boards and placing them across the opening, we drop the rope down the wall.

As quickly as possible I climb over the window ledge and start my slide down to the ground.

As I am half way down the rope, I hear a noise below me. I can see a guard hiding in the murky shadow at the corner of the building.

He runs forward with his bayonet pointing up at me.

I have to scamper up the rope and back into the room as though I am a circus performer.

We close the window, replace the boards and stuff the blanket in the stove.

Just as we lie down, the door bursts open and two new guards enter the room. Using their rifles as clubs, they strike blindly as they run around the room. Calling the interpreter, they ask for the man who was seen crawling out of the window.

No one answers.

The guards are furious! They threaten the group with mass execution if the man does not come forward!

I begin to move; Jack grabs my arm and holds me back.

Silence is heavy as the guards survey the group, trying to figure out what to do with us. They turn and leave, slamming the door behind them.

We hear them striding into the guards' room where loud voices follow their entrance.

After an hour we relax and know that nothing will be done to us tonight.

The smoldering stink of the blanket is overpowering but we dare not open the window.

Jack and I discuss our error of not investigating the possibility of an extra guard at the rear of the building. We hadn't noticed any before and so deduce that he has just been stationed there this evening. We figure the guards were doubled because of the increase in artillery action in the distance.

"Damn it," I growl, "they expected some of us would try an escape soon and they anticipated the very night we would try. Geez, if only I hadn't been incapacitated yesterday, we could have made it. Now we have to discard our whole plan because you know they will be watching us very close from now on."

The pangs of hunger are rewarded as Jack suggests we eat a small portion of our bread supply to allay our sinking spirits. I am for the idea.

While nibbling on the hard sour bread, I think of all the things that have happened to me since my capture. An hour ago I was sure of escape and eventually leaving all this behind. Now I know we are in for a long time and many more things will probably happen.

My physical condition is going down hill every day.

I guess my weight at approximately one hundred and thirty pounds. My arms and shoulders are still sore and stiff but I know they will be better in a few days.

I am not so sure about my back. During work yesterday I felt sharp pains jabbing around my hips, in the small of my back and down my legs. Something is definitely wrong back there. Probably x-rays and chiropractic treatment will be necessary to straighten it out.

My feet and legs are numb up to the knees and it feels as though I am walking on stilts. I can feel no contact with the ground and I stumble quite often.

As I think about these things, I make up my mind: I will not let them get me down. I will stick it out to the end when I know liberation will come. I have too much to live for. Life holds too many wonderful things for me to give up now!.

Thinking of my condition brings thoughts of Roger.

"I wonder how he is? Is he still alive? Did they actually take him to a hospital as they promised?"

I pray to God for help and ask Him to watch over me and help me to live through this torturous hell.

Chapter Eleven

Early the next morning the guards enter our room as usual to wake us. But instead, they order us to gather all our possessions and form out in front in five minutes.

Confusion is everywhere as we collect our helmet liners and tin cans; our total belongings! Until last night, it included a blanket.

As we huddle in a tight group before the schoolhouse, the wind pierces us with knives of icy steel. It is bitter cold and the snow driven by a winter gale, stings our faces.

The Brute calls the interpreter, who informs us, "We will be moving to new quarters. We will have regular meals, hospitalization, beds, church services and no work."

It sounds like heaven to us but we know better than to believe them. All we can do is follow the guards and hope for the best.

The interpreter continues, "The Brute wants to inform you that we will meet trucks later and then be driven to our destination. However, for now, we will walk."

Laughter greets this last statement and we proceed down the road and take our leave of Heidweiler. This German village has been home to us for over two months and now it seems like we are leaving an old friend behind.

The ranks are buzzing with conversation. Rumors fly wildly. Even "Kilroy" couldn't go to all the places that are mentioned.

After the first two hours the group is all talked out and we save our strength for marching.

Wading through the new fallen snow saps our limited energy. Our shoes are soaked through to our frozen feet. Out pant legs are frozen stiff up to the knees and make an icy noise as they rub together.

The next four days melt quickly into one torturous nightmare of forced marching. There is no let-up either day or night. We are given nothing to eat and the only water we have is from the snow we melt in our mouths.

The guards have been changed twice and only The Brute remains with us. He evidently is in charge of the captives and will stay with us until we reach our destination. The march is beginning to tell on him also but he is in good physical condition. He has food and proper clothing. Also his sense of duty to his country seems to help him keep going.

We have marched continually for ninety-six hours as the fifth day dawns.

Finding ourselves just outside a small village, we ask for a rest break and are told we will rest in the town.

It has stopped snowing and the dawn is beautiful as the sun rises over the snow covered roofs of the houses. Everything is smooth with Winter's white blanket. Here and there a horse drawn sleigh slips along the icy road. Smoke curls slowly upward from the stucco chimneys and the warmth from them would be a God given mercy, but it is not for us.

We cannot enjoy the beauty of the scenery because our bodies are exhausted and our eyes bloodshot. Except for a few detours around craters in the road, it is not visible that war's destruction has even touched this village nestled against the hillside.

By the time we march safely inside a courtyard, similar to the one in Heidweiler, the day is bright and the sun begins to warm us with its shining rays.

Our pant legs begin to thaw and the soggy OD's cling to our cold skin. The courtyard gate is locked behind us and all but one guard enters the house. We assume they are getting a hot meal alongside a warm stove.

Jack and I stumble up to the side of the barn and find a dry board to rest on. Sitting dejectedly, we discuss our future with hoarse voices.

Torn dirty clothes cover extremely thin bodies that are topped by heads of bearded skeletons. Weary arms extend down through worn jackets and end in bony claw-like hands. Only remotely do we look like we are related to the human race.

A shuffling, stomping noise in the barn catches our attention. We are sure there must be cows inside that may provide us with a meal and possibly heat for our cold bodies. Edging toward the door, Jack and I slip inside. The heated stench makes us nauseous.

Quickly grabbing a milking stool from the wall, I sit down to the cow nearest the door. Jack is standing by the window with one eye on the guard and the other on the can I am filling. When I hold it up to him, he hands me his can and I fill it with hurried jerky motions. It

171

tastes like food for a king and soon we empty two more cans.

Since our shrunken stomachs can hold no more, we scout around inside the barn for more food and find potatoes in the feeders.

Taking the cows' meal doesn't phase us. They will get more tonight. The milk tastes good so we drink another can, not thinking if the cows are diseased or not.

Other prisoners have also guessed what the barn holds. Soon it will become noticeable to the dozing guard that his prisoners are all disappearing into the barn. He knows we cannot escape over the high walls and even if we could we are too tired to go far.

Jacks stops all of the prisoners trying to enter and only lets in the men who know how to milk a cow.

Soon five of us are steadily milking and the "whang-whang-whang" rhythm of milk squirting into cans sets a din inside the steamy, stinking barn. Two men are busy by the door gathering full cans and handing them outside with a potato underneath.

After about ten minutes the door to the big house opens and the guard is relieved. The new guard takes his position and after lighting up a cigarette, glances in our direction then settles down to wait for the other guards to join him.

In a short time the cows are dry. They begin to stomp their feet as they step from side to side trying to resist our efforts to strip milk when there is no more. The supply of potatoes has also given out and so we leave the warm barn to join the other men outside. Even though the warm milk and raw potatoes have given them relief from hunger and cold, the prisoners still look half dead to me.

With a fresh change of guards, we leave the quaint village that contains a barn full of dry, hungry cows.

We are stiff from sitting during the rest period and the first few miles are torture to our aching muscles. Soon the muscles are flexed enough to stop hurting but they are giving in to sheer exhaustion again. It is a matter of keeping my mind on my movement and I must remember to put one foot forward, then the other.

I find it a queer sensation to know parts of my body are freezing and yet sweat stands out on my forehead.

My nerves are frenzied by my constant commands to move; unconsciousness would be bliss.

At noon we are joined by new details of prisoners being moved out of small villages where they were also forced to work. The group now totals over two hundred men, all in the same physical condition.

It is becoming quite evident that some men will not be able to march much longer. They stumble and fall, continually being helped to their feet by their buddies. It cannot last; no food, no water, no sleep. Something has to change.

The number of guards is not increasing with the influx of new prisoners and it is evident the prisoners are weighing the possibility of a revolt. The guards' rifles are off their shoulders and are being carried in a ready position with bayonets attached. Some men are grumbling and trying to organize a resistance but to no avail. We are too far gone to make any quick movements.

Two men on the edge of the group pass out; their frail forms twitching with convulsions as their bodies refuse to go any farther.

The Brute is notified. He stops the entire mass of prisoners. Striding back along the road side, cursing because of the delay, he kicks the bodies furiously and orders them to rise. They are beyond responding and are as near death as humans can be without their souls leaving to be with God.

We watch. Two hundred grim men who are too deadened to do anything.

The Brute points his rifle at the back of one man's head and fires, spilling blood and splattering brains over the trampled snow.

We are instantly shocked and move toward The Brute.

The guards fire into the threatening horde and twenty more men drop in screaming agony.

We draw back to the middle of the road in terror as we ponder the cruelty we have just seen.

Calmly lighting a cigarette, The Brute calls for the interpreter.

With pain in his voice, Schmidt echoes the words, "The same fate awaits any of us who drop out of the march. There aren't enough guards to leave with the men who pass out, or can't make it."

The Brute is enjoying his cruel notoriety.

As we slowly move away from the horrible massacre, Jack says, "The man who passed out but wasn't shot..." he pauses for a breath, "I hope he is dead."

I look at him with a shocked face. "What a revolting thing to say!"

"But I do hope he is dead," he answers quietly. "If he should come to and see the bodies around him and figures out what happened, he could go insane."

Without a word I agree with Jack and I wonder if it wouldn't be better to be dead than going through this march.

Then it finally dawns on me; this march is a means of killing us off before we are liberated!

Suddenly the roar of an airplane overhead breaks the stillness of our snow deadened foot-falls. Glancing up, I can see the plane swing to the right, circle, and swoop down on us with machine guns rattling.

It's an American P-51 and the pilot's aim is as good as he had been trained. Men drop like ten pins before the deadly fire. We fall over each other trying to escape the line of lead that is digging up the snow in front of us. Screams and curses mingle with the roar of the plane as it circles back for another pass over us.

We stand up in the ditches and wave our arms and helmet liners frantically.

The pilot must think we are German infantry and will not be discouraged from his mission of death. Two more passes completely unnerve us as we scramble farther into the open fields to escape.

I bury my face in the snow and pray as reverently as I ever have. When I finish praying I raise my head to find the plane has left. Death is everywhere.

The guards are on their feet and are regrouping the men. As they come to a still body, they jab it with their bayonet to see if it is alive. The dead are forgotten and the wounded who cannot walk are left to suffer and take care of themselves.

Jack is by my side.

We move on leaving fifty men by the roadside. Our group now numbers less than one hundred forty, reduced by the wantonness of war.

174

Late in the afternoon we are joined by other prisoners and are marched through the night. By morning our number has swollen to over five hundred.

The men are dropping out from exhaustion and never an hour passes without four or five shots being heard. Some men who have passed out are being carried or dragged on blankets by their buddies.

Jack and I have made a pact that if either of us falls, the other will help until we both can no longer go on. This gives us a boost and we know we will try to outlast the other so as to be the one helping instead of the one needing help.

Seven more days go by.

Jack and I figure we have walked over a couple hundred miles. It is a walk of zombies now. Death lurks behind every tree along the road. The branches seem to reach out with devil's spears to knock us down.

At noon on the next day we approach another small village. In peace time the scenery would be breath-taking but in our condition we can see no beauty. Our eyes are almost blind from the glaring snow.

The men have been throwing away clothes during the march just to lighten their weary bodies. They will freeze during the cold March nights yet sweat blood during the warmer days.

We enter the village and find ourselves being herded into another courtyard. This one is more like a military marshaling area with no barns or cows.

We sit in the snow to groan over our miseries.

Within ten minutes the silence is broken into pandemonium by the shouting of guards.

We hear the running of feet as a man is being pursued around the house that sets in the middle of the courtyard. He runs past us and drops a large round loaf of bread into the lap of a man and cries hoarsely, "Hide it!"

The guards sprint around the corner of the house just as the loaf is covered by a mass of arms and legs. They roar by us and around the far corner of the house.

By this time, the pursued has dropped to a sitting position among the men and is unnoticeable.

High pitched German voices scream at the five hundred men, cursing us because of their frustrated chase.

Again the interpreter is called forward and the guards scream orders at him.

Turning to face us, he loudly proclaims, "Some lucky SOB swiped a loaf of bread and these bastards are really 'teed' off."

The motions he makes with his hands and face gain the guard's approval. They nod their heads believing the interpreter is giving us hell and the man who stole the bread will soon be found.

The interpreter continues, "Now listen, men, they have threatened to shoot some of us if we don't turn over the thief. I say, that's tough! It looks like we're going to die anyway, so some of you might just as well get some good from the food. Don't give the man away! Whoever has the bread, enjoy it and don't think of the threat. Let the bastards know we can stick together too."

The guards are smiling. They cannot understand a word of English and they still think the interpreter is giving us hell. Now they are telling the interpreter to order the thief to stand up.

He repeats the order to us.

Five hundred men rise to their feet and stand waiting defiantly.

Surprised beyond all belief, the guards turn on their heels and leave the area.

Loud and raucous noises follow their retreat.

The thief back-tracks to the spot where he threw the loaf and joins those around it in a feast of warm fresh bread. Jack and I are near enough to hear his story but not near enough to get any of the bread.

It seems he wandered away from the rest of the prisoners when he entered the courtyard and came around the other side of the house. Passing by an open basement window, the fragrance of freshly baked bread drew him to follow his nose to the source of the heavenly aroma. Peeking down, he saw a middle aged German woman taking loaves of bread from a huge oven and stacking them on shelves in the middle of the floor. When her back was turned, he saw he could reach in and get one but only if he had a long pole. Looking around, he spied a pitch fork under the porch and eagerly grasped it.

Upon returning to the window, he waited for the baker

176

to turn her back and then reached in as far as possible. He still was a few inches short and then looked for another pole. Under the porch he found an old broom. While keeping an eye out for the guards, he removed a shoe lace and bound the two poles together. He crept out from under the porch and went back to the basement window. When the proper moment arrived, he threw the weapon like a spear. Making contact, he began withdrawing it.

Just then she turned around and a loud scream broke from her lips. She fled upstairs with one long continuing wail of fright.

At the very moment he got his hands on the bread, the guards rounded the porch and he turned the corner. That's when we first saw him. His story gives us a laugh and revives our morale.

An hour later we are on the road again with a fresh change of guards, except for The Brute. He is still with us. We mull over the possibility that he still may be with us when we are liberated. His brutality fills my mind and revenge entertains my thoughts for the next few hours.

We are repeatedly being bombed and strafed by our own planes. More men are dead on the road with the snow soaking up their bright red blood. Others are shot for falling out of line, their grotesque bodies sprawled like shadows beneath the trees.

Three days later the guards halt our death march at the entrance to a huge barbed wire fenced area.

It is Stalag XII, located at Limburg.

I am so engrossed in watching my feet and trying to keep from stumbling that I am not aware we are nearing it until we stop.

Guard towers dot the fenced camp. Search lights and machine guns can be seen inside the tower windows. Guards pace back and forth on the catwalks around the outside.

The towers are thirty feet in the air and their position commands every inch of the inside of the camp and the outside surrounding area.

The huge gate opens, bidding us to enter and join the thousands of other prisoners already within its confines.

We pass through three barbed wire fences before

entering the actual camp site.

Marching to the center, we can see buildings that house the prisoners of every nationality; English, French, Canadian, Polish, Russian, Turkish, Indian and many more. They seem content in their compounds.

Another huge gate bars our way and before we can go through it, we must be thoroughly searched.

It takes hours.

When the gate finally opens we find we are in an American sector that comprises about one-fourth of the camp. The Americans do not seem content to just lie around like some of the other prisoners. Hustle and bustle is everywhere: some are washing clothes in pails of water, others are selling their field jackets for shoes and other things. Some men are doing mild calisthenics while others just walk.

We are herded into an empty barracks and told to call it home. It is bare inside: four walls, small windows, a leaky roof and an uneven cold cracked cement floor that is wet and covered with filth.

I figure it is over one hundred feet long and forty feet wide. When all of us are inside and try to lie down, we are cramped for space. Only by crossing over others legs, can we stretch out. Soon the snoring of exhausted men fills the early evening.

Jack turns to me and quips, "And we walked over three hundred miles for this?"

"Yeah," I answer sleepily, "I guess our truck reservations were canceled."

In the morning we are free to move around our barracks. There are four of these huge buildings bursting with American prisoners. I guess the total number to be about four thousand, and this is only in one section. There are numerous sections filled with American prisoners, stretching for hundreds of yards. And this is only one camp!

"I wonder what the total number of American prisoners amounts to? Think of the thousands who were killed in the death marches, gas chambers, massacres and those who froze or starved to death. Then there are those who were killed by our own planes because the Germans wouldn't mark the camps and marching columns with large POW signs."

Jack listens as I continue, "What good are rules when there is NO WAY to make countries keep the rules? Why not make just one rule. No Wars!"

"Good idea," Jack mumbles. "But probably there would be a country who would break that rule."

"Yeah, but in a way we have benefited by Germany breaking some of the rules of the Geneva Convention."

"How do you figure that, Bob?" Jack questions.

"Well, they weren't supposed to take medics and chaplains prisoner but by doing so we have some medical treatment and spiritual comfort."

"Hey, that's right! I heard that Sunday we are going to celebrate a Mass here in the barracks because we have a Catholic priest," Jack says.

He is correct. On Sunday morning the barracks is crowded to standing room only. Outside the men are standing in silence, clear to the fence. They will not hear a word of the Mass but they are a part of the event.

Jack and I have not moved outside since yesterday afternoon, knowing if we do our places will be swallowed up by the eager men who envy our positions in the blessed barracks. A Spiritual communion is taken by all. It gives new life to us and strength to bear the burdens that are mounting.

Daily the war activity is increasing.

Chapter Twelve

Jack and I lie side by side on the cold cement floor.

The air is filled with the stench of too many unwashed bodies and too few accommodations for their normal function. Diarrhea is prevalent and accidents are common.

From the middle of the barracks a man cries out in anguish as he stumbles over the tangled mass of prisoners and realizes he is too far from the doorway and the cans outside that are provided as latrines. Curses emit from the men in the path of the unfortunate wretch as he leaves a trail of excrement when he tumbles over them.

The doorways and the immediate area around them are crowded by men who know enough to stay close to the latrines. Seldom do they find them unoccupied and it is a gamble being so close to the doorway. In the morning they are the first ones called by the guards to clean up the filthy mess made by those who could find no place but the ground.

The evening has brought our ration of bread and water to nourish our wasted bodies.

"From what the men in the other barracks say about conditions here, our stay isn't going to be too pleasant," Jack announces as he slowly chews his bread.

"No," I answer, "and from what we've seen so far I have no reason to disbelieve them."

"Well, at least we are here with thousands of others and that's sort of a safety net."

"Yeah, but remember the other prisoners told us the guards are ruthless and brutal. Just as soon shoot you as look at you. All it means to them is another cleaning detail for their rifles."

"We also have to remember they told us the men nearest the guards are always picked for the work details. It doesn't matter if you just came off a work detail or not," Jack reminds me. "They beat the hell out of you if you protest."

"It's bad enough to have to live like pigs, but not being able to systematize work details will make our life horrible, especially considering our physical condition," I add.

The cold from the cement floor penetrates our weary bodies as we drop off to a fitful sleep.

It is common knowledge that in the morning we may find we have been sleeping next to a dead man.

Death hangs over the camp twenty-four hours a day and picks its victims at random from the crowded quarters. Each day the numbers increase. These lifeless bodies are not through with indecency even in death.

In the early morning Jack and I watch the death patrol as it enters our compound with its awesome wagon. Prisoners pull it through the opened gate and stop in front of our barracks. We can see the stripped bodies of the dead being loaded on the wagon; their skeleton forms grotesquely covering others.

"What do they do with the bodies?" Jack asks the man standing silently next to him.

"They're thrown in mass graves without any semblance of church services or record of death," he pronounces quietly and then he continues. "Their number is not even noted, and when this is all over, grave inspection teams will have to count the twisted skeletons piled one on top of the other. Even then it will be just an estimate."

"Geez," Jack mutters, "and to add to all that confusion will be the sorting of Americans from the French, English and all the other nationalities. Thousands in a grave will make it an impossible task."

"There are still a great many to join the dead," I think as I watch the wagon leave our compound with its ghostly load.

I cannot speak. I join Jack as we sit by the side of the building soaking up the heat from the March sun. Only by looking at the sky can we see anything clean and beautiful.

After a while I look at the men in the compound milling about and it brings me back to reality.

A great number are stripping their clothes off and ridding themselves of body lice that have infested the camp. An attempt is made everyday to have the prisoners do this but it is an empty dream. Some men are so slovenly they won't join in the task and since the lice multiply rapidly in this filth, we can only hold our own against them. There comes a peace of mind in knowing that we are at least trying.

A commotion is going on at the fence that separates

181

the first barracks of Americans from the Indians.

Jack and I stand up to see what is happening and we join the crowd walking in that direction. Any change in the monotony is welcome even if it sometimes means trouble for others.

It seems that a trade is being made by an Indian offering a sweater for a pack of American cigarettes.

"How does he expect anyone to get his hands on a whole pack of cigarettes?" I ask incredulously.

One enterprising G I takes him up on his offer and the Indian finds the pack only contains sticks. He is not only furious, he has lost his sweater.

Calling out his charges at the G I, brings more Indians from their barracks and a small riot is soon halted by a thin fence and the thought of the machine guns on the towers.

This ends the trading for the day but it will start again tomorrow.

Once a week, we are told, a Red Cross Parcel is split between eight men and the cigarettes are very valuable. If saved for a few days, a cigarette can be traded for a ration of bread. This seems unbelievable but it is true.

Some men have matches and others have cigarette lighters with lighter fluid in them. Where these articles come from and how the prisoners manage to hang on to them, mystifies me. I know it will do no good to question these men about their source of supply.

Jack and I ask questions about the possibilities of escaping and find it quite impossible.

We are almost in the center of the camp and the search lights illuminate the area thoroughly. Even if we did reach the edge of the camp, after passing through numerous compounds, we would still be faced by three tangled barriers of barbed wire, one of which is supposed to be charged with electricity. Rumors have it that huge dogs prowl between the outside fences. These dogs are said to be vicious and trained to attack and kill a man instantly.

Tunnels have been attempted but no one talks of them for fear of passing out too much information and attracting suspicion.

If there are escape exits, we have not been able to locate them.

Several escape stories are often repeated.

It is told that three men took a scarce amount of lime that is used in the latrines and mixed it in some way and painted a white stripe down the road. As they came to the gates, they motioned for them to be opened and then proceeded to "paint" their way to freedom.

Another story is about the surveyors. Seems they rigged up an instrument that looked like a surveyor's transit and they "surveyed" themselves down the road to freedom.

Others tried to hide in the wagons leaving camp but were always caught by probing guards. Some even faked death to ride on the death wagon out of camp. Outside they were thrown in the mass graves. Their problem became one of surviving in the cruel German winter without clothing. Yet, men will do almost anything to escape the hell we are living.

Some of us concentrate on passing the time as quickly as possible.

Papers from the Red Cross Parcels are torn up to make decks of cards and checker boards. Bits of iron torn from the buildings are fashioned into horseshoes and great competitions are aroused.

These few entertainments are zealously guarded as they can not be replaced.

Details are always working while recreational activities are going on. Some men have to work all the time and some have figured the guards out and never are in the wrong place when the details are needed. It takes an active mind to be on the lookout for these things. Self preservation is foremost in our daily lives and we know no one will look out for a man that does not look out for himself.

During the night the roar of airplanes overhead is continuous and their nearby falling bombs gives us the knowledge that the Allies are winning this war.

As soon as the bombers leave, we fall asleep, only to be awakened by a flashlight shining in our eyes, a club cracking our ribs and the guards shouting, "Raus! Raus!"

Jack and I are on a work detail!

All night we fill bomb craters at the railroad yard.

On succeeding nights we find that when a light shines in our face, we automatically get up and start moving.

We're not fully awake but we know instinctively that we better start moving toward the door or a brutal beating will be meted out by the large clubs the guards carry.

Filling bomb craters and clearing railroad yards of tons of debris is a nightly task now. Hundreds of us are made to work under the watchful eyes of the guards who never hesitate to beat a man for stopping to catch a breath.

It is useless work. Night after night the planes come over and the railroads are put out of commission. For our efforts we are given an extra drink of putrid water when we return to camp in the morning.

Each day brings new columns of prisoners. The camp is filling to three times its capacity and the new men are quartered in the open, sleeping on the frozen ground with no blankets to keep them warm. Pneumonia is raging throughout the compounds and new death wagons are added to the Death Patrol to carry away the fortunate unfortunates.

Jack and I stay together continually. We talk of home and loved ones. By now we know all there is to know about each other, our families, our homes, our town and our thoughts. We discuss the current events and the build up of men in the Stalag. Soon the Germans will have to think of something to relieve the burden of the overcrowded camp. We wonder what they will do.

We don't have to wait long to find out.

As we are discussing it, the guards enter the compound and through an interpreter explain that the camp is too crowded and some men will have to be moved to a new camp. One hundred will be able to go from our compound each day.

Jack and I look at each other. Here it is again; another of their extermination plans. Some of the men crowd around the guards to be chosen for the select one hundred.

"How can they be duped into this? They should know by now that any of their promises only means death!"

We sit and watch the men leave. Each day for a week a hundred from our compound are taken to the main camp road where they are joined by thousands of others and then are marched away.

I wonder, "Will they ever be found after the war?"

184

"Maybe as ashes in crematoriums or piled high in gas chambers," Jack answers.

The stench of unburied bodies fills the countryside and we think of all the terrible things we have heard that the Germans do with prisoners.

It is the middle of March 1945 and both Jack and I feel the war is rapidly coming to an end. The Germans are disorganized and their military strength is being crushed by the Allies. I pray for God's help and ask Him to spare me from making the wrong decision that could lead to my death.

On the seventeenth of March our compound is emptied and we are placed at the head of a long column at the main gate.

My legs, feet and back are paining me to the extent that I cannot stand upright but it is not noticeable in this group where everyone is in the same condition.

As the march starts we are led to the railroad yards and jammed into boxcars. They are the small type similar to the French 40 et 8.

Seventy men are packed into one boxcar with Jack and me. We immediately sit by the wall near the sliding doors and fight to keep our position from pushing, hysterical men.

There is not enough room for everyone to sit down and fights break out even before the doors are slammed shut and locked.

For hours we sit in the boxcar, not moving. No latrine facilities are provided and a stench begins to fill the car with unbearable odor.

Suddenly we are jolted by an engine coupling onto the boxcars. Slowly, slowly we move over the repaired rails and broken ties. We pick up speed as we go out of the railroad yard. Less than a half hour later we stop.

The engine uncouples and chugs away.

We figure we are on open tracks that the Germans are willing to sacrifice. When we hear the planes overhead, we realize we are in unmarked boxcars and are targets for our own planes.

Our fighters come over. Their attack is deafening. Lead rips up and down the boxcars, killing, tearing and punching death into men like rain.

Screams of agony and fright fill the boxcar accompanied by the well know whistling of rushing air that is followed by earth shaking explosions of bombs. Men stampede where there is no room to move.

It is over in a few minutes and our boxcar is still teetering precariously on the broken track. We hope it will tip over and break open so we can make a run for it.

I realize that Jack and I are clinging to each other and only the pain of his fingers digging into my shoulder brings me back to reality. As I release the hold on his shoulders, I feel the pain leave mine.

We sit and wait.

I experience a terror so appalling that it takes all my mental ability to remain sane. I want to shriek my way out of this hell but Jack puts his hand over my mouth. I have been screaming. This world is so horrible my mind is whirling and I doubt the memories will ever leave me.

Although I cannot see in the pitch black, the scene stands out as if it were well lit, burning on my brain.

The wounded and frightened men scream. Some men are running the length of the car, crashing into each other and tumbling down on those sitting or lying. Fists fly. Vulgar oaths pour out into the boiling cauldron of this human hell.

Jack and I are crouching against the wall, covering our heads with our hands. We pull our knees under our chins to protect our swollen legs and feet from the men who are running back and forth.

Some men are completely out of their minds, babbling on and on. Others are crying to God for mercy.

Time passes. We wait.

A minute, five minutes, an hour!

We stay close to the wall, tense, motionless and waiting for the next signal of death. It comes all too soon.

The same thing happens over and over again for seven long days.

We don't know how we can possibly still be alive. God must be looking out for us even though He lets us endure this chaos. He guards us from physical death yet we die a thousand mental deaths this last week.

I pray constantly and only in this way am I able to

withstand the pressing, pounding, whirling in my mind. It seems as if I am on the verge of blowing my top and going out of my mind. I pray and wait. The balance swings like a pendulum and I fight a mental breakdown. I pray some more.

Many in our boxcar are dead. Some are wrecks of human forms, having been reduced to this state before by months of torturous living. This new ordeal could not be withstood by them. Some are unconscious from shock, exhaustion or the anger of those who went berserk This unbelievable madness is beyond my imagination.

During the constant strafings and bombings our boxcar still stands upright. There are bullet holes spattered on the roof and sides like a full starry night.

I work a spike loose from the flooring and drill a small hole through the sidewall just above my shoulder. It lets in a small beam of light. We press our mouth to it and draw in a breath of clean, fresh, sweet air.

· The seventh day is like the rest, except the stench is worse. The dead are rotting among us and the filth of human excretions covers everything and everyone. We are degraded to an inhuman level, where death is preferable, yet we live. Live? We are merely existing. A group of chemicals compounded with souls that refuse to leave and go to our heavenly rest.

Jack and I lean against the wall and each other for support. We are numb and yet pain racks our dehydrated, swollen bodies. Our tongues and mouths are dry and cracked. To speak is impossible. A hoarse whisper takes all our strength. The moaning has ceased and only the heavy labored breathing of a few, breaks the silence.

By turning slightly I can see through the hole I have drilled. The view is limited to an area of only a few feet. My vision has deteriorated from being in the darkness to a point where the light blinds me completely. Only by squinting can I see vague images outside. I am realizing what Hell must be like.

It is torture not to be able to see the outside surroundings and enjoy nature's beauty. I vow to remember these days with all the things that have happened and then give glory and praise to God for helping us. I tightly hold on to the rosary that is wound through my fingers.

As dusk falls on the seventh day, the sound of German voices outside brings us out of our stupor.

The lock on the boxcar door creaks. The noise of the door rolling open frightens us with thoughts of new ordeals. A helmeted German head pokes inside and yells, "Raus! Raus!"

It takes a full minute to convey the message from my brain to my legs. Only by crawling am I able to reach the door. To the amusement of the guards, I topple to the ground in a heap. Jack's body plummets down alongside of mine and the Germans drag us to the bank of a small creek that was formed by melting snow.

Three other prisoners join us.

We five are the only ones living out of the seventy-two men who entered our boxcar a week ago.

Our jackets, shirts, pants and underwear are stripped off roughly by the guards and the filthy clothes are thrown aside. We feebly rinse our faces, hands and bodies in the icy water and we tremble from the shock of the cold wind. G I pants and jackets that show heavy wear are given to us. They must have come from dead prisoners.

I try to drink the cold creek water but the pain in my throat stops me so I only rinse out my mouth.

As we look up we can see the derailed, blasted train. A few cars are burning with their human contents locked inside. Other boxcars are bombed hulls and the ground around them is strewn with bodies. The cars that have rolled over have bodies protruding from the sides.

Each atrocity seems more horrible than the last. We want to cry but tears will not come.

Hundreds of boxcars that filled this area are now reduced to a mass of twisted broken forms: coffins for those who died inside. The few survivors that slowly move among the destruction look like ghostly shadows hauntingly guarding their former friends.

We are gathered together at the edge of the rail yard and given a cup of hot gruel. It burns our parched throats as we force it down.

Later we spend the night on the frozen ground resting for a march they say will begin in the morning.

It is March twenty-fourth, three days before my twentieth birthday.

I think, "I am not old enough to vote or buy a drink, but maybe when I have aged a little and seen life and have made my own decisions, then maybe they will let me be treated like a man." The irony of it brings a wry smile to my lips. I feel as though I have already lived through a lifetime.

Regularly throughout the night I massage my legs and feet. They are numb and yet a throbbing pain constantly pounds in them. The huddled forms of the other prisoners are sprawling out on the ground looking almost peaceful.

I wince and think, "Well, one more ordeal over. How many more to go?"

I thank God Jack is still alive. We need each other so much if we are to survive.

In the early hours of morning, we are stumbling along the road again farther into the heart of Germany. Small groups of prisoners join us at each mile and soon our number must be over a thousand. I know that it will dwindle as the day wears on and the overpowering exhaustion takes its toll.

It doesn't take long before the rifle shots at the sides of the road tell us there are some that will never march again.

For four days we march down slippery hills and through the sloppy valleys. Only two things change: on the third day we are given a slice of bread to eat. It sickens us and brings on convulsions to many. The other change is an American liaison plane flying over.

It's being used as an artillery spotter. It flies so low we can see the smile on the pilot's face as he waves to us. We know he is not far in front of our advancing lines and we wave and shout, somehow expecting him to stop and pick us up and fly us to an American hospital with clean sheets, medicine, food and writing paper.

"Writing paper!"

That reminds me, "My family doesn't know where I am! They probably have received telegrams listing me as 'Missing in Action.' That is all they know!"

The idea of them actually believing me to be dead has not, until now, entered my mind.

"How does it effect my mother? Is she reconciled to the fact that she now has only three sons instead of

189

four? What's happened to my two older brothers who are also in the Army? How have they fared? What about Jean?"

I look at the mark her ring has left on my finger.

"Will she be waiting for me?"

These thoughts bring tears to my eyes and a new surge of power to my body. "I have to live through this nightmare to find the answers to these questions. I have to ... I have to ... I have to!"

Jack lays his hand on my shoulder and croaks, "What are you mumbling about?"

He must think I have finally slipped into the snake pit with my incoherent words. Knowing full well the wild look in my eyes betrays me, I look at him and repeat, "I have to live through this to find the world I once lived in."

He understands and we mechanically stumble down the road that seems to have no end.

Chapter Thirteen

The morning of March 29th, 1945, one hundred and one days after my capture, dawns in its bleak greyness and finds me cold and miserable.

It is difficult for me to distinguish between the dead and the living as I lie shivering in the snow. The guards are moving about and their shouts of, "Raus! Raus!" stir the men into action.

Yesterday the liaison plane passed over our column which numbers approximately five hundred men.

As we walk out of the area this morning, we leave behind those who have died during the night. The thirty or more dark forms lie in grotesque shapes in the snow, scattered among the empty bedding imprints of those who have survived another night.

There are mixed emotions within our group. Some of us praise God for keeping us alive through the night while others wish for death to take them out of this misery. Some are openly contemplating suicide by falling out of line so they will be shot. Others have taken this means to end their suffering. Today there will be more.

Jack and I lean on each other for support during the first mile. Finally our stiff muscles start working more freely and we sway from side to side by ourselves as we plod on.

"Remember our pact," I recite to Jack, "if one of us goes down, the other will carry him."

"Yeah, Bob, I'll remember," he wheezes.

Neither of us wants to be carried, so the thought of our "pact" gives us more determination to stay on our feet.

Less than an hour passes before the first shots are heard. Though they sicken us, we cannot muster the strength to react in any way to the finality of their echoing report. The guards will not let the march be delayed for any reason.

"Pray, Bob, pray," Jack hoarsely whispers through parched lips.

"Yes," I answer, "we can go farther if we keep our wits. Do you want a drink of water? I've melted some snow in my can under my jacket? Here, at least wet your lips."

The cold water dribbles from the corners of his mouth

and freezes in his beard. The shock of the cold water revives my deadened thoughts as I too sip from the can. Clouded eyes peer through metal frame glasses that set like frozen barbs upon my nose.

Though I know I am surrounded by hundreds of men, I do not see them nor feel their presence. I can only concentrate on keeping my balance and placing one foot in front of the other. I am aware of my heavy breathing and the lack of strength in my body. Thoughts float in and out of my consciousness making me barely aware of my situation.

A prisoner in front of me falls to the rutted road and does not move. For a split second I am stunned as my path is blocked. I stumble a few steps to the right and my way is clear. I continue to plod on.

Sharply, close behind me, a rifle fires and awakens my mind. "The fallen man has been murdered." I cannot turn around. I must keep moving. I only know that Jack is stumbling along beside me. His words again encourage me.

"Pray, Bob, pray."

Before noon, just outside a small farming village, the prisoners begin to talk among themselves. They want to revolt!

In the distance I can hear rumbling motors of vehicles which I think are tanks. And here we are walking away from them!

Suddenly, as if by a unanimous vote, everyone of us sits down in the middle of the road. We refuse to walk another step.

The guards are furious and use their rifles butts to gash skulls and break ribs. We still refuse to move.

I cover my head with my arms and pull my knees tightly under my chin. I pray for God's help. My eyes are closed. My body is tense as I wait to be brutalized by the guards. A rifle butt jabs fiercely into my back, knocking me over into the snow. The pain is excruciating.

"Raus! Raus!" yells the infuriated guard. "Schnell! Schnell!"

Again he strikes me, this time a glancing blow to the head. The noise it makes on my helmet liner rings in my ears. I lie still with muscles tense, eyes closed, fully expecting another blow or kick from his heavy boot.

After a few seconds, I know he has forgotten me and is venting his anger on the next man.

I dare not move. I must not open my eyes. My breathing is shallow. The yelling of the guards and the thuds of the beatings fill my ears.

Other prisoners are screaming in pain. Their agony is shared by all of us.

A hand pushing on my shoulder, alerts my body to another blow. My muscles draw tight in response, awaiting the attack. It doesn't come.

"Bob? Bob?" shouts Jack, "Are you alright?"

Slowly I open my eyes and glance up before lifting my pain filled head. Pandemonium surrounds us.

Jack retrieves my battered helmet liner and hands it to me. As I reach for it, the movement sends an alarming pain through my back where I was clubbed. Very carefully I gain a sitting position and hold my breath as the pain subsides. Jack is examining me with his eyes, searching for the answer to his question.

Again he asks in a much quieter voice, "Bob, are you O.K.?"

"Yes," I hiss through clenched teeth. "I just don't want any more of this. Damn, I'm sore. It hurts to breath. Thank God for these tough helmet liners."

The roar of an airplane above us does not stop the wild disorder. Our liaison plane is circling the area as if drawing attention to itself, will bring us relief.

Jack points to the houses at the edge of the village and the white sheets that are hanging from their windows.

"They're signaling defeat, Jack! They're surrendering!" I scream.

Tanks with motors roaring are fast approaching the far side of the hill. Their monstrous metal tracks create screeching sounds as they pass over a rocky area.

The guards are at the peak of their ferocity.

"Hang on, Bob. Pray! Something has to break. We may end up in the middle of a battle right here. Lie down! Don't move."

I can see a horse drawn wagon coming down the road from the village. Its driver is a woman holding up a white flag high in the air. The horse is frightened by the activity and the woman is pulling hard on the reins to control the skittish animal.

Our plane continues to circle above us. I can see a helmeted head with goggles peering down as the pilot banks sharply in his turn.

The guards have stopped their brutal actions and gather on the far side of the prisoner column. They are wildly gesticulating, rifles held high, feet firmly planted, and they are shouting at each other.

The horse drawn wagon stops at the side of the road in the midst of us.

Steaming kettles of hot cereal are uncovered and while the woman scoops it into our rusting containers, she points to some milk cans. We pour the cool milk over our cereal.

Greedily we drink the tasty mush. Its warmth is felt as we gulp it down.

Jack and I push ourselves away from the wagon, holding our cereal cans tightly. As we reach the fringe of the crowd, we can see the guards. Some of them are smashing their rifles on the road and sitting down near the prisoners. Other guards join The Brute as he makes a dash for the nearby woods.

"What the hell does he think he is going to do, fight the tanks?" I ask Jack in disbelief.

"Guess so. Doesn't look like he is going to surrender."

Our liaison plane signals the direction of the tanks as they crest the hill less than a mile away. Helmeted crewmen can be seen peering from their open hatches. The deep rumble of motors fills the air and joins with the tumultuous confusion of our cheers.

With immense feelings of gratitude, we run down the road on legs that moments ago could hardly walk.

Spreading out over the fields, the tanks maneuver a flanking position. We run to them, tumbling and falling at every step. A discord of voices holler and sing, tears pouring from our sunken eyes. The tears dam up in our matted beards which refuse to part and let them fall. We hug each other and dance together as the tanks come abreast of us. Hundreds of us kneel. Bare headed, we bow. I have my rosary in my hands as I give thanks to the Lord for our liberation.

I see men clamber over the tanks, pleading for food. Husky tankers throw crates of dehydrated food to them. The crates are broken open with strength of crazed, starving men. The contents are fought over like hungry dogs. Quickly the cans and boxes are opened and the contents devoured, killing some prisoners as soon as they are liberated.

Jack and I sit on the bank along the road, munching on a D bar. The taste of chocolate gives us a feeling of quick energy. But we realize we must not gorge ourselves on this rich food, so we enjoy its creamy goodness, slowly nibbling and treasuring our possession of it.

A convoy of soldiers in G I trucks pull into the area. They dismount quickly and position themselves around our perimeter.

A Captain asks for information.

Hearing about The Brute and his followers, he details a squad to follow two tanks and go after them.

The rest of the guards sit patiently under the watchful eye of the G I's.

From the road we can see down into the valley where The Brute has entered a patch of woods. The tankers close their hatches and quickly make their way in pursuit. The rattle of machine gun fire is answered by the short burps of the German arms. The tankers are not impressed as they continue downhill, firing into the woods. The soldiers leave the tank's protection and zigzag to the sides, surrounding the Germans.

It only takes a few minutes to overcome them. No German prisoners are taken. The G I's have seen the massacres along the road behind us and they have no love for the Germans at this moment.

One of the German guards left for the village before the tanks arrived and is now returning, riding a bicycle.

"Evidently he doesn't want to walk back to the rear prison camps," I suggest.

The former American prisoners do not give him a chance to plead his case. The bicycle is rammed over his helmeted head which now protrudes through the wheel spokes. The roar from the onlookers fills the countryside with a deafening sound.

195

Jack sums up the situation. "He has made us walk all this way and we sure don't want to take the privilege of walking back, away from him."

The German guards are searched and relieved of their army equipment except what is necessary for their survival on the march to the rear of the Allied lines. There are eighteen guards, the same number that survived in my company when we were taken prisoner. I feel no compassion for them as they are marched back down the road.

"At least they will be fed!" Jack mutters.

Our dead and wounded are loaded into the trucks.

The G I 's that occupied the seats have entered the village and have secured it. We are told that we will be leaving in an hour.

"What do you say, Jack, let's go into the village and see what's going on?"

"I'm game," he answers.

Though our steps are slow and deliberate, we are able to walk into the cluster of houses without incident.

"Look over there," Jack exclaims, pointing to a building where a large swastika is fastened over the door.

"Must have been an officer's quarters," I guess. "Come on, let's take a look."

Boldly we mount the porch steps and push open the door. German paraphernalia is scattered on the floor.

"Looks like they left in a mighty big hurry," Jack laughs.

Pictures on the wall of dour faced officers peer out at us as if they resent our presence. Dishes are on the table, set for six. An overcoat is draped on a bench and a pair of rubber boots neatly stand at attention next to the desk.

"That trunk looks interesting, Jack."

"Yep, let's see if it's locked."

The lid opens easily and our eyes feast on a wealth of souvenirs. Stacked in the top compartment is a row of German medals. Next to them are a box of cigars and two bottles of cognac.

"Let's see what's under this," Jack exclaims in enthusiasm.

"Damn, look at that, will you!" I yell. "A gold handled parade knife."

There are bayonets in oiled scabbards, fur covered back packs, elaborate leather belts, officers caps and shoulder insignia.

Quickly I fill one of the back packs with an assortment of items, hiding a bottle of cognac in the bottom. The bayonet in its scabbard is inserted along the side, its handle protruding out of the top.

"We better get out of here before one of our officers comes along and confiscates these," I whisper.

Peering out the doorway, we do not see any soldiers in the area. Furtively we make our way off the porch and down the street.

"How are we going to hide this stuff from the other prisoners?" Jack pants.

"Wrap it in your field jacket," I whisper back as if the walls of the houses and the trees along the road might hear and discover our booty.

Nonchalantly we join the group of former prisoners and within minutes we are loaded into open trucks. The motors roar as the drivers gun them before shifting into gear. A cheer breaks out from the men as we slowly move into line and proceed down the road. No one dares voice a complaint when our aching bodies are jolted about as we pick up speed on the rutted road.

"Looks like we made the right decisions, Jack. We survived!"

We are sitting next to each other on the hardwood seat of the truck, leaning forward, our pack sack on our lap covered with our field jacket and protected with our arms.

The wind whips a liberator's blanket around our shoulders, giving us some protection from the freezing weather.

My thoughts now are of home and that joy of anticipation brings a smile of happiness. There is peace in the hearts of the men as we realize the torture of the German guards is over.

Each of us sits quietly, hands clasped in our field jacket pockets for warmth.

We sway back and forth with the movement of the truck. Our minds are too busy to look at the countryside as we travel up steep hills and down into secluded valleys.

Since we do not pass any American units or equipment for the first few miles, we theorize the tanks must have broken through the German lines and dashed cross country, led by the liaison plane, to liberate us.

"Hope we don't run into a German ambush," Jack says. "They didn't send much fire power along with us."

"True," I answer, "but I've seen our liaison plane in the distance a few times. He must be searching the woods ahead."

"Hope so," Jack's muffled voice states through his blanket covered mouth.

A deep hole in the road jolts us from our seats and the scramble to regain them occupies our thoughts for the moment. "That's just God's way of reminding us that we are riding and not walking," Jack quips.

Hours later, bruised and tired we reach Leige, Belgium, where we are checked into a field hospital.

"A hot shower! Geez, I haven't had a shower in over three months!" I laugh as the medic hands me soap and a towel.

"Well, it'll wash off the delousing powder. And a good G I haircut will help also. After your shower, you can shave and we'll have clean clothes for you too. They'll assign you a bed in a tent over there," he nods toward a huge canvas enclosure across the field.

"What about my back pack?" I ask uncertainly.

"Don't worry about it. Hell, I've seen so much stuff, I don't even bother looking at it anymore," he chuckles. "But if it will make you feel better, I'll look after it while you shower."

Slowly I nod my head. "O.K. I'll pick it up on my way out."

The shower feels wonderful. As I soap up for the third time, letting the hot water relieve my muscles, I cannot help but yell out, "Hooray, I'm free!"

My legs are weak and I have little feeling in them below the knees. A clean bed where I can sleep sounds like something out of a dream.

The medic hands me the back pack after I've donned clean pajamas and a robe. Before going to bed, he diverts me to the mess hall where other prisoners are gathering.

"Damn, this G I bread tastes like angel food cake

to me," I laugh with my mouth full. "And this milk tastes like it's all cream."

We must look ridiculous to the husky K P workers with our gaunt faces which appear even more sunken once we shaved. Boney faces and crane-like necks show out of the neckline of the pajamas that hang on our thin bodies. Clawlike knobby fingers clutch at the bread as we layer a thick spread of butter on each slice. White feet, the color of transparent alabaster, are removed from our shower slippers as we unconsciously rub them together to revive the circulation, only to find pain instead.

The happy talk that pours from our cracked lips reveal to the mess hall workers that we are strong enough to overcome the frailty of our bodies. They serve us quietly and efficiently as they listen to the stories being recalled.

Later, as I lie on my bed, a stretcher placed across two saw horses, I wonder which tent Jack is in. A medic enters and administers a shot of vitamins and a shot of penicillin into by scrawny buttocks. Sleep comes quickly between the clean white sheets.

In the morning, awakened by a blaring loudspeaker, whose harsh tones reminds me of the "Raus! Raus!" of the guards, I roll off the stretcher and grope my way out into the main aisle. There I realize where I am and sheepishly return to my stretcher. I notice others are confused and quietly returning to their warm beds. We are told not to get up as this area is for non-ambulatory patients only.

Breakfast in bed!

I am being served breakfast: juice, oatmeal, toast and coffee with cream and sugar. I can't believe it!

The medic sidles up to the side of my stretcher, a chart in his hand. "Roll over, soldier, here comes the needle again," he orders.

"This is the only part of being liberated that I don't like," I mutter.

After shaving and having the bedding changed, I lapse into sleep again, only to be wakened by Joker shaking my shoulder.

"Hey, Jackson, you got it made here. How you doing?" he asks.

"O.K. I guess, but I keep having my sleep disturbed

by some medic with a needle and loud bastards like you," I answer with a laugh.

"Guess what, Jackson? My brother is a medic here! Just couldn't believe it! He's getting off duty now and we're going to have a drink."

"Drink of what?" I ask, "Milk?"

"Hey, here he is now."

After the introductions and comparing the brothers who look like twins, though one is much thinner, I again ask, "Drink of what?"

"Oh, our usual, rubbing alcohol and pineapple juice. That's all we can get our hands on out here."

"Wait a minute. Joker, hand me my back pack and don't try any funny business," I laugh. Taking out the bottle of cognac, I hand it up to Joker. "Here, enjoy this and pass a few snorts to the other medics for being so good to us." Their happy faces are more than enough to repay me for the bottle. I have a drink with them before they leave.

Every four hours the medic returns with his chart and needle. My body is responding to the food and rest but after three days the pain in my legs and feet is excruciating. They are frozen. I cannot walk.

On the fourth day, as a stretcher patient, I am flown by hospital plane to the General Hospital in Paris.

As I am being taken out of the ambulance by German prisoners who work for the medical transportation unit, the ambulance driver warns me, "Hey buddy, hang on to the stretcher. These guys have been known to dump patients."

"Thanks."

Reaching behind my head and pulling the bayonet from the back pack, which I'm using as a pillow, I wave it in front of the stretcher bearers. "Let's go, boys. Raus! Raus!"

I can hear the ambulance driver laughing as I receive a very smooth ride up the steps and into the hospital where I am carefully deposited in a ward overflowing with former prisoners, all needing medical and surgical attention.

Jack was not on the plane with me but I know he is in good hands now.

I am given a cursory physical exam and asked alot of questions by a doctor wearing Captains's bars.

"How long have your legs been in this condition? Do you have any feeling beside the pain in them? What are these bruises on your back? Where did you get this gash on your head? You say your back and hips bother you; how long has this been going on? Do you know what caused it?"

As I answer the questions I must relive the past three and a half months. It brings back alot of horrible memories.

I am put on a high calorie diet with four meals per day and snacks whenever I wish. Vitamins and antibiotics are administered every four hours. I must report any change in the condition of my feet and legs. "No, you can't have a pass to see Paris.!"

Writing paper is supplied to me and my first thoughts are of Jean and my mother.

Sitting in a wheelchair as I mail the letters, I pause to think of the answers I will receive. "Will everything be as I left it? Are my brothers and mother still alive? Will Jean still be waiting?" The happiness of liberation is tempered with these questions but I must wait for the answers.

Back in bed again, I find even simple exertions tiring and sleep comes easily. I do not fight it. The doctor has said, "Rest and a proper diet is what you need for now. We must build you up again."

After a week of lying in bed with daily visits from various doctors, I am taken by wheelchair to a private consultation room. The ward boy tells me the doctor will be here in a few minutes.

A middle aged Colonel dressed in white enters the room, a stethoscope dangling from his neck and a set of gold "chickens" on his shoulders. He does not smile as he leafs through my chart.

"How do your legs feel this morning, soldier?"

"They hurt like hell, Sir."

"Do they feel any better today than they did a week ago or do they feel worse?"

"Worse, Sir."

"Can you walk at all on them?"

"No, Sir."

"Get up and try. Walk to the table."

201

Pain throbs in my feet as I attempt to stand on them. I cannot feel contact with the floor and I stumble to the examining table.

"Let me help you up on it," he grumbles.

After thoroughly examining them by bending my knees, poking needles here and there, probing at my toes and pinching my skin, he enters the information on my chart and assists me to my wheelchair.

"I'm afraid we have no other choice but to amputate," he states matter-of-factly.

"WHAT!"

"We can't wait any longer for circulation to start. Gangrene will set in."

We stare at each other eye to eye. The thought is incredulous to me.

"You want to cut off my legs!" I scream.

"It's the best solution."

I am unwilling to believe what he has told me.

"There have been hundreds of others before you in this same condition," he continues, his voice controlled.

My emotions are not controlled and I hear my voice shouting, "Well, that's not the best solution for me! If I have to use a cane, I'll use it. If I have to have crutches, I'll use them. And even if I have to sit in a wheelchair, I'm going to look down and see my own feet in my shoes!"

Calmly he looks at my raging face and then sternly asks, "You realize you can be court-martialed for refusing a government recommended operation, soldier?"

"Well, you can just start the court-martial now," I state firmly. Then leaning forward I look him straight in the eye and scream, "And you can stick your government recommended operation up your ass, COLONEL!"

The consultation is over!

For the next two days my routine does not change: examinations, vitamins, needles, good food, sleep and pain.

On the third day blood samples are taken and there is no sign of gangrene in my leg and feet tissue. The nurse while washing my legs remarks, "It will take a few more washings before these lines on the back of your legs are gone."

"What lines?"

"Well, they look like the lines doctors make to mark where they will cut when they begin surgery."

"Well, there won't be any surgery on me!" I state firmly.

"I know," she answers with a smile while continuing the bath. "Everyone on this floor knows!"

"You mean it has been confirmed?"

"Well, yes, according to your chart. But I'm sure the doctor will tell you that during his rounds today."

When she is gone, I twist my legs into a position where I can see the lines. The line on my left leg is just below the knee, while the line on my right leg is midway between the knee and ankle. Quickly I tuck the blanket over them and lie down, thinking how close I have come to losing my legs.

In the afternoon, while dreaming of the future, a patient walks up to the foot of my bed and stands smiling at me.

It is Roger!

"Rog, you ol' son of a gun, how are you?"

His firm handshake brings tears to my eyes for more reasons than one.

"Bob, I've been looking all over the place for you for two weeks. I never really expected to find you but I just had to keep looking."

He sits on the edge of my bed. Our words won't come. It's just like it was when he left over three months ago.

"So they really did take you to a hospital?" I muse.

"Yep," he smiles, "in a truck! When I was better, they started marching us back to work and then the G I's liberated us."

"Sure am glad to know you're O.K., Roger," I marvel. "I'm leaving tomorrow."

"Leaving tomorrow?"

"Yeah, I'm being Z I'd. Zone of Interior."

"Back to the States?"

"That's right. I guess I'm in for a long recuperation with these legs of mine. I shouldn't kick though, I guess."

"What do you mean, you shouldn't kick? It's not your fault..."

"I mean I'm pretty lucky so far. They told me this morning I can keep my legs."

"Keep your legs! You're kidding?"

"No, I'm not kidding. It has been touch and go for the past week but it's O.K. now. They want to get me back to the States where they can give me the full treatment. Therapy, you know."

"Well, I'm sure glad for you Bob, I'm sure glad. Have you .. ah .. received any .. letters yet?"

"Nope, not even a 'Dear John.'"

"Well, she'll be waiting, don't worry about that."

Roger stands up and straightens my pillow before saying, "Good bye."

The two medics that carry my stretcher from the ambulance onto the hospital plane are commenting on my weight.

"About a hundred and fifteen pounds, I'd say."

"Naw, you're way off, a hundred ten at most."

I laugh, "That's close enough, boys, it's really one thirteen and I've put on a few pounds in the last two weeks."

They are still arguing as they leave the plane for another patient.

The converted C-47 has permanently installed stretchers along the walls. I am next to a soldier who does not smile as some of the rest of us. There is an empty place below his right knee under his blanket.

Our first stop is the Azores, where I ask for a banana and I make it last half way to Mitchel Field in New York.

We are told we can go forward to the cockpit, one at a time to view our flight. I choose to be last.

Shortly after I am helped forward, I can see the New York skyline and the Statue of Liberty. What a thrill.

Circling, before landing, I can see crowds of people lining the field's fences.

We land and taxi by the waving masses and do not stop until we are a hundred yards from the ambulances. The door is opened and we can hear a military band playing in the distance.

Medics in full dress uniforms enter the plane and transfer us to new stretchers. Then two by two we are carried down the ramp and paraded in front of the flag waving crowds.

A speaker is blaring and exhorting them to buy war

bonds!

We are being used as bait to excite them, goading them into doing their patriotic duty.

I am furious! So is the patient in the stretcher next to me. We do not want sympathy. We just want to come home and be treated in a hospital so we can recover.

Without a word, we both crawl from the moving stretchers and holding on to the edge of them, we hobble to the waiting ambulances. The officers waiting for us are angry, very angry but the crowds cheer louder.

We are home!

In a waiting room in the terminal, I hold onto the door of a telephone booth and place a long distance call.

The operator breaks the silence. "Ready on your call, Sir."

"Jean?"

"Yes, .. is .. is that you Bob, my darling ..?"

The End